UNMASKING NARCISSISM

UNMASKING NARCISSISM

A GUIDE TO UNDERSTANDING THE NARCISSIST IN YOUR LIFE

Mark Ettensohn, Psy.D.

ALTHEA
PRESS

For general information on our other products and services or to obtain technical support, please contact our Customer Care Department within the United States at (866) 744-2665, or outside the United States at (510) 253-0500.

Althea Press publishes its books in a variety of electronic and print formats. Some content that appears in print may not be available in electronic books, and vice versa.

ISBN: Print 978-1-62315-642-8 | Ebook 978-1-62315-643-5

Contents

Foreword *7*

Introduction: More than a Myth *10*

PART 1 The Grandiose Dimension *33*

1 A Grandiose Sense of Self-Importance *36*

2 Personal Exceptionalism *44*

3 Arrogant, Haughty Behaviors and Attitudes *53*

4 Dealing with Grandiose Behavior *62*

PART 2 The Self-Serving Dimension *73*

5 A Strong Sense of Entitlement *76*

6 Lacks Empathy *85*

7 Is Exploitative of Others *95*

8 Dealing with Self-Serving Behavior *106*

PART 3 The Vanity Dimension *121*

9 Preoccupation with Fantasies *124*

10 Requires Excessive Admiration *135*

11 Feelings of Envy *145*

12 Dealing with Vanity *153*

Conclusion *164*

References *170*

Resources *176*

About the Author *177*

Index *178*

Foreword

Many people know the term *narcissism* comes from the tale of Narcissus, the Greek youth who fell in love with his own reflection. Still, many are unsure how to identify narcissism, and perhaps most importantly, how to live with it when the disorder has an effect on them. What's important to first understand is that, unlike the handsome and vain Narcissus, a true narcissist doesn't really love himself; rather, he suffers from a lack of an authentic self.

People who tend toward narcissistic personality disorder (NPD) did not develop a healthy sense of self-esteem at a critical age. Whether the fault of caregivers who were unable to provide "empathetic attunement" to their young child, or the result of another trauma, the consequences are that narcissists believe they must be beautiful, smart, talented, and admired. Narcissists are often high-achieving individuals who possess a constant need to prove themselves to gain love—and to compensate for the lack of it in their childhood. As children, many people with NPD had to present an image of perfection, beauty, and success. As a result, they wear the mask of a false self, afraid others will perceive these feelings of inadequacy through their disguise.

No matter how difficult those with NPD may be to relate to, it's important to note that the dynamics resulting in troublesome behaviors, such as the constant need for admiration and assurance, the lack of empathy, and the arrogance and vanity, are simply unconscious attempts to maintain a false self. After feeling that their true thoughts and feelings didn't matter, narcissists may fear for their psychological survival and become preoccupied with having their needs met and their feelings understood or "mirrored."

When you understand the roots of NPD, you can learn to alter the dynamics of a difficult relationship between yourself and someone who exhibits narcissistic tendencies. In this book, you'll gain tools to transform your relationships, with the goal that you can become your own advocate, rather than try to change the narcissist. While the natural tendency may be to confront a narcissist about their offending behavior, this tactic has poor results and reinforces the narcissist's feelings of victimization. The best strategy is to make the narcissist feel wanted and appreciated. Meeting negativity with more negativity fuels the narcissist's need to defend. Instead, defuse the interaction by acting on insight and attempt to make your own needs known in a calm, nonconfrontational way. When dealing with a narcissist who knows no boundaries in his demands, make space for yourself by saying "no" in a kind manner in moments of calm. Issuing ultimatums and blame may be a relief in the moment, but it will ultimately put you in a hard position. There's one exception: when dealing with a "malignant" narcissist who may be dangerous, your only course of action may be to exit the relationship. Don't tolerate exploitative and abusive behavior, or become swept up in polarized thinking. The narcissist can both idealize and devalue those involved with him, and you don't want to be caught up in either mental state. The goal is to move back into the middle ground, keeping sight of yourself, your sense of worth, and your own needs.

Your loved one, friend, or coworker may always be a narcissist, but there are ways to heal—even if it's just within yourself. Once you understand the root of his or her behavior, you can begin to act upon it in a healthy, calm way and create a better environment for everyone. I urge you to use this book as you travel the path toward healing. Perform the exercises and use the tools presented within to help you survive and thrive during the ups and downs of difficult interpersonal relationships.

—Jane Simon, M.D., New York, New York

More than a Myth

Narcissists tend to be treated with disdain. The common stereotypes are that they are selfish, arrogant, and entitled predators who use people up and throw them away without a second thought. Search online for advice on how to deal with a narcissist and you'll be buried in an avalanche of articles that all basically say the same thing: leave. Narcissism is so maligned that you would be hard-pressed to find more than a handful of contemporary writers willing to say anything positive about individuals with narcissistic tendencies. To call someone a narcissist is tantamount to calling him or her a jerk. Numerous sources support this point of view.

This book, however, is not one of them. This book is written from the perspective that narcissists are human beings. Odds are, you're reading this book because you want to understand the narcissist in your life and learn better ways to relate to them. Maybe you're at your wits' end dealing with a boss, a family member, or a romantic partner and want to learn how to think differently about that person's behavior. The aim of this book is to help you understand the psychology of narcissism so that you can build better relationships with yourself and the people in your life.

To understand narcissists, you must first empathize with them. It's easy to write off a difficult person as bad, broken, or evil, but doing so just doesn't get anyone very far. Instead, it's necessary to put yourself in that person's shoes.

Empathizing with a narcissist isn't as difficult as you might think. The core pieces of narcissism are common to everyone. You know what it's like to want other people to like you and how it feels to be misunderstood. You know the experience of not measuring up to another's expectations. You've been angry with someone for not considering your feelings, and you've been envious of someone because they had something you didn't. These are some of the thoughts and feelings that lie at the heart of narcissism and motivate narcissistic people.

Ultimately, narcissism isn't really about loving yourself too much. It's about not having much of an authentic self to love at all. The qualities often associated with stereotypical narcissism—selfishness, arrogance, and entitlement—act as armor, protecting the vulnerable and fragile person inside. By learning to see past this armor, you can learn how to have a better relationship with that person.

What Is Narcissism?

The word *narcissism* comes from the ancient Greek myth of Narcissus, a young man who was tricked by a spirit into falling in love with his own reflection. He became so obsessed that he eventually died from starvation. Tragically, Narcissus never realized he was in love with a reflection, not a real person. He died attempting to obtain perfection.

But the tragedy doesn't end there. There's a lesser-known character in the myth named Echo, a nymph with a peculiar curse: She could only repeat what others said to her. She couldn't share her own thoughts and feelings. One day, she saw Narcissus walking in the woods and immediately fell in love with his beauty. Although she tried to get his attention, her curse made it impossible for her to communicate. Narcissus only heard his own words echoed back. Echo's tale also ends in despair. Eventually, she died of a broken heart.

The story of Echo is familiar to anyone who has been in a relationship with a narcissist. You try to make yourself known, but your efforts seem doomed to fail. You seldom (if ever) feel seen or understood. Your perspective is ignored, and your feelings are invalidated. Like poor Echo, your attempts to communicate fall flat. At times, you feel invisible, enraged, depressed, and humiliated. You become locked in a battle for recognition. While the narcissist gazes longingly at the mirror, you gaze longingly at the narcissist. But unlike the simplicity of a Greek myth, real-world relationships with narcissists cycle between highs and lows. Sadly, you experience Echo's rapture and despair over and over as the relationship shifts between periods of idealization and devaluation.

So what, exactly, is narcissism? The term has a long and muddy history. A century ago, it was used to describe a form of male sexual perversion. Since then, the word *narcissism* has meant many things, including a stage of psychological development, a way of relating to others, a form of self-esteem regulation, a character trait or style, and a personality disorder.

Today, *narcissism* is a term most commonly used in the context of narcissistic personality disorder (NPD). Personality disorders are characterized by enduring personality traits that cause problems in people's lives and relationships. In the case of NPD, these problematic personality traits revolve around the issue of self-esteem. Unlike more focused disorders such as phobias or panic attacks, personality disorders typically affect many areas of life. Personality disorders may require long-term treatment and can cause complications like depression, anxiety, and substance abuse.

Recent research analyzing scores on a popular test for measuring narcissism, the Narcissistic Personality Inventory (NPI), suggests that unhealthy narcissistic traits can be divided into three dimensions: a grandiose dimension, a self-serving dimension, and a dimension based on vanity. This book is organized using these three categories as guides.

How Is Narcissism Diagnosed?

In an everyday clinical setting, NPD is diagnosed after a thorough diagnostic interview, during which the treating or diagnosing clinician takes a full history of the patient. Clinicians may use information from a variety of sources to make a diagnosis. These can include the patient's history, input from loved ones, and even how the clinician feels sitting in the same room with the person. Therapists spend thousands of hours sitting one-on-one with people who have all sorts of mental illnesses. Over time, they become quite sensitive to how it feels to talk to someone with NPD. Often, this sort of information is valuable to the clinician because it can reveal material that the patient is either unwilling or unable to report.

Psychologists also use a resource that classifies mental disorders called the *Diagnostic and Statistical Manual of Mental Disorders* (DSM) which is published by the American Psychiatric Association. In each edition of the DSM, diagnoses are refined, discarded, or revised according to current medical and psychological knowledge. The fifth edition of the DSM (DSM-5) was published in May 2013 and contains over 200 specific, diagnosable mental disorders. Disorders in the DSM-5 are defined based on commonly co-occurring symptoms. Other criteria are also considered to rule out competing diagnoses.

According to the DSM-5, to be diagnosed with NPD, a person must exhibit behaviors and attitudes that include a grandiose sense of self, little empathy for others, and a

How Are Symptoms of NPD Measured?

In research settings, narcissism can be assessed using tests that are designed to measure certain personality traits. Some are focused on grandiose narcissism, like the Narcissistic Personality Inventory (NPI), while others are focused on vulnerable narcissism, like the Hypersensitive Narcissism Scale (HSNS). Since these assessments measure theoretical aspects of narcissism, they typically aren't used for diagnosis. There are some assessments that can measure narcissistic traits for the purposes of diagnosis, but they often require special training to interpret. These include the Minnesota Multiphasic Personality Inventory, 2nd Edition, Restructured Form (MMPI-2-RF), the Millon Clinical Multiaxial Inventory, 3rd Edition (MCMI-III), and the Rorschach Performance Assessment System (R-PAS). While assessments like these can provide valuable insight into a person's personality, diagnosis should always include a face-to-face clinical interview by a qualified professional.

persistent need to be admired. Nine specific personality traits are considered to reflect narcissism, broken up here into the three dimensions mentioned earlier. To be diagnosed, a person must exhibit at least five of the personality traits. Of course, it is always best to consult a professional for actual diagnosis.

The Grandiose Dimension

Traits in this dimension reflect a need to feel important, special, and better than others.

1   Has a grandiose sense of self-importance. The person may exaggerate her accomplishments, expect recognition for minor achievements, or expect special treatment from others.

2   Believes he is "special" and unique and can only be understood by, or associate with, other special or high-status people. The person may consider others to be beneath him, idealize a group of people and long to be accepted by them, or be convinced that he has a hidden talent that is waiting to be discovered by the world.

3   Shows arrogant, haughty behaviors or attitudes. The person may act as if she is better than others, treat others with derision or contempt, or appear overly confident.

The Self-Serving Dimension

Traits in this dimension reflect difficulty considering other people's feelings and a tendency to take advantage of others to meet emotional needs.

1   Has a sense of entitlement. The person may have
    expectations that others will make unreasonable
    sacrifices to accommodate his needs and desires.

2   Lacks empathy. The person may have difficulty
    seeing other people's perspectives and considering
    their feelings.

3   Is interpersonally exploitative. The person may take
    advantage of others, leaving them with a feeling of
    having been used.

The Vanity Dimension

Traits in this dimension reflect self-absorption, self-
admiration, and a tendency to envy others who have qualities that the narcissist wants.

1   Preoccupied with fantasies of unlimited success,
    power, brilliance, beauty, or ideal love. The person
    may talk often of finding a perfect job, giving a per-
    fect performance, or finding a perfect mate.

2   Requires excessive admiration. The person may
    regularly fish for compliments and may feel slighted
    or insulted if she doesn't receive enough praise.

3   Is envious of others and believes others are envious
    of him or her. The person may envy others who he
    believes have talents, abilities, or other attributes
    that the person wants.

You may find that some of these traits apply to a loved one you hadn't previously considered narcissistic. You may even find that some of them apply to you. If so, don't worry. Everyone exhibits some of these traits from time to time. Nobody is perfect. Occasionally, all people are prideful, envious, and subject to periodic lapses in empathy. When you think about narcissism, it's helpful to think about a continuum of traits (such as a thermometer), rather than a hard and fast dichotomy (such as an on/off switch). Looking at a thermometer, problems only start when the temperature reaches an extreme. Similarly, when a person is too high on the "narcissism thermometer," problems inevitably result.

Everyone Started This Way

Narcissism isn't inherently bad. Everyone passes through an intensely narcissistic phase of development. Without at least some narcissism, nobody would have any self-esteem. Feeling proud about an accomplishment or thinking that your new haircut looks good are everyday examples of healthy narcissism. In its most general sense, *narcissism* just means *love of self*. As Whitney Houston famously said, that's "the greatest love of all."

Narcissism has long been written about as something positive that only occasionally becomes a liability. Sigmund Freud identified narcissism as an important process in which young children learn to feel good about themselves. In the decades that followed Freud's early work exploring the concept of narcissism, the idea gradually evolved into a cornerstone of human psychology.

Freud's Seminal Paper, *On Narcissism*

In his 1915 paper *On Narcissism*, Sigmund Freud distinguishes between primary narcissism, a normal part of early development in which the child is fixated on his or her self, and secondary narcissism, when the self-obsession of early childhood extends into adulthood. In the early part of the 20th century, the field of medicine was very concerned with understanding disorders that cause a person to lose touch with reality (e.g., schizophrenia). Neurologists like Freud wondered what could cause such a severe breakdown in the mind's ability to tell fact from fantasy. Freud theorized that secondary narcissism was the cause. He believed that the person could not distinguish fantasy from reality because his libido was too attached to his own self.

The last 100 years of psychological and neurological research have brought with them new insights into brain-based causes of illnesses like schizophrenia. Nevertheless, Freud's ideas still have value because they point to the importance of narcissism in the early history of psychology.

Primary narcissism is the term used to describe the ways that very young children seem to feel invincible and omnipotent, as if they magically create the entire world every morning when they open their eyes. Children know nothing of the work that goes into parenting. From the child's perspective, caregivers miraculously appear whenever he or she needs something. This creates a feeling of safety and trust. Without primary narcissism, nobody would ever feel safe enough to take their first steps. In time, a child's primary narcissism is thought to change into a more realistic sense of his or her limitations. This opens the door to the child's understanding that he or she needs others for care and protection. At a certain age, children will run away from their parents with gleeful abandon, never thinking to look over their shoulder to see if mom or dad is still there. After a few tumbles, scares, and skinned knees, children become much more cautious. They realize that the world is big and scary, and that they are not self-sufficient. Understanding, on an emotional level, that you need others is the foundation of the ability to experience feelings like guilt, dependency, and love.

More recently, research has identified two basic dimensions of human psychology: (1) the need to have a stable and positive sense of self, and (2) the need to have satisfying relationships with others. Another way to describe the first dimension—having a stable and positive sense of self—is *healthy narcissism*.

When You Just Can't Leave

If you look up "advice for dealing with a narcissist" on the Internet, you'll find an endless supply of articles telling you to leave the relationship. Sometimes, that's excellent advice. Leaving may be your best option if the relationship is abusive or unsafe.

But what if the narcissist in your life is someone that you can't leave? What if it's your parent, coworker, or boss? What if it's an ex-partner with whom you are co-parenting a child? What if it's someone you love and you're just not ready to throw in the towel? Is it possible to work toward a better future for the relationship?

The short answer is yes, it's possible, but it isn't always successful. Personality disorders are very difficult to change. It takes years of hard work and the person must want help. Some narcissists fall into the "wanting help" category, while others spend their lives blaming others for their own problems. Read this book to understand narcissistic behavior, gain strategies for healing yourself, and learn tips for extinguishing or avoiding hurtful encounters, but do not use this book if your sole intention is to change someone else's behavior.

Because narcissism is such an important idea in human development, much time and attention has been devoted to understanding what happens when narcissistic development goes off track. What happens when those early experiences of omnipotence and self-sufficiency persist into adulthood? Moreover, how does it happen? These are the questions that have kept generations of psychologists up at night.

Types of Narcissists

The history of narcissism is long and complicated. A central piece of that history is a famous disagreement between two theorists who specialized in treating narcissism.

Otto Kernberg developed a theory that views narcissism as fundamentally pathological (i.e., development took a wrong turn). His basic idea was that narcissism develops when very young children are denied certain needs for care and affection during important periods of development. Having their needs denied causes frustration that interferes with normal processes of maturation, resulting in defensive self-sufficiency and narcissism.

Unlike Kernberg, who thought narcissism was a case of development taking a wrong turn, Heinz Kohut believed that narcissism was more a case of development getting stuck on the path to maturity. Kohut's ideas revolve around how children use their caregivers and friends to build stable and healthy self-esteem. When children don't receive the type of time, care, and attention needed to accomplish this task, they become stuck in immature ways of getting self-esteem needs met.

The debate about whether narcissism is the result of a developmental detour or a developmental delay has raged for decades. Some consider it to be irresolvable. However, psychologists and researchers noticed that Kernberg and Kohut actually seemed to be describing different groups of narcissists. Kernberg's group was more openly arrogant, vain, and entitled, while Kohut's group seemed more sensitive and depressed.

This realization has led researchers to identify and validate that there are, in fact, two types of narcissists. Since this represents a developing area of psychology, there isn't an established terminology to describe these groups. Some of the terms that have been used include overt and covert, thick-skinned and thin-skinned, oblivious and hypervigilant, and exhibitionistic and closet. This book will use grandiose and vulnerable to describe these two types of narcissist, as these terms highlight some defining features of each group.

For those of you familiar with the Disney movie *Beauty and the Beast*, the characters of Gaston and the Beast are perfect examples of grandiose and vulnerable narcissism.

Grandiose Narcissists

If you've seen the film *Beauty and the Beast*, you know the villain, Gaston, is arrogant, vain, boastful, and manipulative. He is completely full of himself. In the Broadway musical version of the story, his character even has a song titled "Me." Gaston feels entitled to "the best" in everything, and exploits others to get what he feels he deserves. He prides himself on his beauty and abilities as a hunter and ladies' man. However, without these attributes, he doesn't have much of an identity. One could say that Gaston's sense of self is dependent on being held in high esteem by others. Gaston is a grandiose narcissist.

Vulnerable Narcissists

In contrast to Gaston's boastfulness, the Beast is quiet, sad, and sensitive. He used to be beautiful, but now he believes that he is ugly. He spends his days protecting a withering rose that represents his last opportunity to regain the ideal self he feels he has lost. A tattered picture of himself as a young prince hangs on the wall—a reminder of the person he once was. Like Gaston, the Beast's sense of self depends on being beautiful and desirable to others, but unlike Gaston, he feels that he has lost these qualities. The Beast is a vulnerable narcissist.

Two Sides of the Same Coin

Gaston and the Beast represent two sides of the same coin. It is often the case in movies, books, and comics that the hero and the villain are related along some shared dimension. Batman represents the ability to use fear and loss constructively, while the Joker represents the chaos these feelings cause when they're allowed to run amok.

Are All Narcissists Men?

NPD is more commonly diagnosed in men. Traditionally, narcissism has been defined by qualities that were considered essentially male. In fact, an early term for this style of narcissism was *phallic narcissism,* from the Greek root *phallus*, meaning "penis," and coined by Wilhelm Reich in 1933. This style of narcissism was described as "arrogant, self-glorifying, aggressive, competitive, and possessing a 'pseudo-masculinity.'" As cultural values and gender norms have shifted, and as use of social media causes people to increasingly worry about image and engage in self-aggrandizement, narcissism has become more gender neutral. Nevertheless, there is still a gender bias when it comes to common ideas about narcissism.

A similar gender bias can be seen with borderline personality disorder and histrionic personality disorder. Both are more commonly associated with women. In fact, histrionic personality disorder used to be called hysterical personality, derived from the Greek root *hysterikos*, meaning "womb." Does this mean that only women can have these disorders? Not at all. Gender biases are not very helpful when talking about mental illness. Both men and women can be narcissistic, just like both men and women can have depression, anxiety, or any other mental health issue.

Superman represents sacrifice and justice, while Lex Luthor represents greed and cynicism. Harry Potter is protected by his mother's love, while Voldemort is the tragic result of emotional abandonment. Dichotomies like these help people better understand relationships. While separating narcissism into grandiose and vulnerable types may help people organize thoughts on the subject, it is important to remember that real life is always more complicated than fiction. Again, it can be helpful to think about grandiose and vulnerable narcissism as a continuum (thermometer) rather than a dichotomy (on/off switch). If narcissism is a thermometer, then *grandiose* is at one end and *vulnerable* is at the other. A person can be anywhere along the line in between. They can even move back and forth.

The Core of Narcissism

At its core, narcissism is about managing self-esteem. If all goes well, people emerge from childhood and adolescence with an internal supply of positive feelings about themselves, using them to get through difficult times and disappointments. The positive feelings come from years of interactions with important caregivers and peers during development.

There are many ideas about the sorts of developmental experiences that contribute to narcissism. That being said, throughout the literature on the topic there is basic agreement that narcissism occurs when very important needs for care are neglected during critical periods of development. Children can easily be taken advantage of by caregivers. Some theorists write about caregivers who use their young children to gratify their own narcissistic needs—using them as magical mirrors that only reflect flattering images. Others write about failures in empathic attunement. If you've ever confided in a friend and felt that he just wasn't really listening, then you know what failures in empathic attunement feel like.

Narcissists grow up feeling the need to be "just so." They need to be beautiful, smart, and talented; respected, admired, and high-achieving. Their sense of self is based on beauty and achievement. This appearance-based sense of self is sometimes called a *false self*. The false self represents the person that the narcissist feels they need to be to be worthy of care—the person it seems others want them to be.

Sometimes the experiences that shaped a person's narcissism are obvious and undeniable; sometimes, they are subtle. A professor once asked his class to answer the question, "What causes mental illness?" The students wrote the kinds of answers you might expect: trauma, abuse, neglect, poverty. "No," he replied. "Everyday interactions cause mental illness." Even the smallest interactions, when repeated hundreds or thousands of times throughout a person's life, can have tremendous influence on that person's mental health.

Putting It Together

The myth of Narcissus is a tragedy. The poor guy never really had a chance. He was tricked into falling in love with an ideal image of himself—an image that could never love him back because it wasn't real in the first place. Likewise, narcissists are tricked at an early age into believing that they need to be perfect to be loved. One prominent writer on the topic calls narcissists "used children." When children are exploited for their ability to gratify parents, caregivers, and peers, they grow up thinking that is the primary purpose in life.

While other children learn that their feelings are valued and understood by caregivers, narcissists learn to shut down feelings that aren't desirable to others. While other children get realistic feedback from caregivers about their talents and abilities, narcissists are inflated by caregivers' unrealistic expectations. While others grow up with a sense of self that is based on authentic feelings, narcissists must make do with a false self that is based on images of perfection, beauty, and success. Underneath that, there is very little sense of an authentic self.

What is an authentic self? Everyone has one. It is the wellspring of joy and sorrow. The authentic self can be seen in the genuine smile of a small child or a person's deep sobbing at the loss of a loved one. A life lived in connection with this part of oneself is inherently satisfying. The authentic self tells you what you like and dislike. It's the part you use when you "follow your gut" or "listen to your heart." Well-adjusted people are raised to connect with this part of themselves and to build an identity based on the experiences that flow from it. Narcissists, on the other hand, learn at an early age to substitute a false self in place of an authentic self.

It is terrifying to lack an authentic self. You become prone to anxiety and depression. It's like living in a house built over a bottomless pit. The floor is rickety and in constant danger of collapse. Wouldn't you always be worried—always checking, and measuring, and asking for reassurance? Narcissists live in existential terror of the floor—their false selves—caving in.

Whether a narcissist is grandiose or vulnerable depends on how defended they are against this terror. The psychological defenses of grandiose narcissists are strong and intact. They experience very little distress or anxiety. For them, the floor feels pretty solid. In fact, grandiose narcissists may have become so fused with the false self that they may not even be consciously aware of the danger lurking beneath them.

For vulnerable narcissists, the floor feels paper-thin. They may have even fallen through a few times, just barely catching themselves in time. They are sensitive to the slightest creak and the smallest disturbance. They are anxious, scared, and need constant reassurance that everything is not about to collapse. For them, their defenses against the terror of not having an authentic self have broken down. Sometimes, the defenses were never strong in the first place. The reasons for this aren't known for sure. However, my own research into this question supports the idea that experiences of bullying or rejection by peers during childhood may cause the defenses of vulnerable narcissists to be weaker than those of grandiose narcissists.

Why Are People So Attracted to Narcissists?

If it's true that narcissists are actually living in constant existential terror (whether consciously or not), why are people so attracted to them?

Narcissists can be very good at exploiting other people's desires to feel important and special. Narcissists who are high in antisocial traits—being deceptive, manipulative, hostile, or lacking empathy or remorse—may do this intentionally, but much of the time it is not something done with malicious intent. Rather, it is a by-product of the narcissist's own cycles of idealization and devaluation. Think back to the metaphor of the floor built over the bottomless pit. The narcissist wants to feel like the floor is perfectly built and can never collapse. What better way to feel perfectly safe than to ask someone with perfect credentials to come over and inspect it? In this example, you're the inspector with perfect credentials. The narcissist idealizes you at first, thereby giving you the authority to make him or her feel safe and reassured. In effect, you are being used by the narcissist in the same way that a young child might use a parent for reassurance.

Gradually, cracks begin to appear in the narcissist's idealization of you. He begins to realize that you are not a perfect being. This makes the narcissist feel insecure, like maybe the floor could collapse. The narcissist feels betrayed by your failure to remain perfect. He may even become angry with you and start to criticize you for any little imperfection. The narcissist is projecting his insecurities onto you, filling you up with his own bad feelings. You were once perfect, but now you are no good. The narcissist must distance himself from you to avoid feeling like the floor will collapse. All the while, you are trying to understand what went wrong.

As this process unfolds, you start to become desperate to regain the good feelings you associate with being idealized. You become caught in the narcissist's gravity. You are now dependent on the narcissist to make you feel good, worthy, and special, just as the narcissist is trying to see himself as good, worthy, and special. The narcissist gazes longingly at the mirror, while you gaze longingly at the narcissist.

How This Book Can Help

The following chapters will look closely at traits and behaviors associated with narcissism, breaking down and explaining each in terms of what is happening inside the narcissist and in your relationship. They'll also talk through the differences between grandiose and vulnerable narcissists. Finally, this book will cover a number of tips to help you cope effectively. If your partner, parent, coworker, or someone else close to you has been diagnosed with NPD or exhibits narcissistic traits, read on.

1

PART

The Grandiose Dimension

Grandiosity is a shield that protects the narcissist from deeply held feelings of insecurity, inadequacy, and shame. Like dropping sandbags off the side of a hot air balloon, narcissists elevate their own egos by offloading their insecurities onto those around them. The narcissist soars into the sky while others are left holding the dead weight. The narcissistic traits discussed in this part are especially difficult to tolerate because they have the effect of making you feel bad so that the narcissist can feel good.

As discussed earlier, narcissists can be grandiose or vulnerable, depending on how well their defenses are functioning. As psychologist and author Stephen Johnson put it, grandiose narcissists spend more time in a compensated state (i.e., protecting themselves from underlying vulnerabilities and insecurities), while vulnerable narcissists spend more time in a symptomatic state (i.e., directly or indirectly expressing the vulnerabilities and insecurities that lie at the core of narcissism).

For the most part, grandiose narcissists make heavy use of two psychological defenses: denial and projection.

Denial is when a person refuses to include important pieces of information in their assessment of a given situation. Instead of facing an uncomfortable reality, a person shuts her eyes and persists in believing a more comfortable fantasy. Secretly, often unconsciously, grandiose narcissists are terrified that they simply aren't good enough. This fear is so threatening that it triggers the defense of denial. By denying their underlying feelings of insecurity and fear, grandiose narcissists can maintain a more pleasing fantasy of perfection.

In contrast with denial, projection involves unconsciously placing feelings of insecurity and worthlessness onto others, simultaneously allowing a narcissist to get rid of the unwanted feelings and imagine that they are better than the "worthless" people onto whom they are projecting. It's an elegant (if socially irresponsible) solution.

In vulnerable narcissism, the grandiose traits haven't gone away; they are merely hidden. Instead of feeling that they are better than everyone else, vulnerable narcissists typically feel that they *should* be better than everyone else and are simply failing to live up to their potential. The underlying duality of superior versus inferior remains; it's just flipped on its head. The resulting sense of inadequacy still rests on an inflated sense of the narcissist's own potential. Vulnerable narcissists are notorious perfectionists, which is merely a disguised form of personal exceptionalism. The belief that one is capable of perfection is, itself, grandiose.

In essence, grandiose narcissists' feelings of grandiosity are conscious, while feelings like shame and insecurity are unconscious. For vulnerable narcissists, it's the opposite: feelings of shame and insecurity are conscious, while feelings of grandiosity are unconscious. In each group, the unconscious feelings drive the conscious. Grandiose narcissists are grandiose because they secretly feel inadequate, while vulnerable narcissists feel inadequate because they are secretly grandiose.

CHAPTER 1

A Grandiose Sense of Self-Importance

A grandiose sense of self-importance means thinking, feeling, or acting like you're more important than others. It's talking down to people, bragging about your own accomplishments, or consistently putting yourself first. When you witness people cutting in line, interrupting or talking over others in a conversation, or always trying to one-up other people's experiences and accomplishments, you're seeing this trait in action.

Steven's Story

Steven was feeling uncomfortable again. Eric, the director of his play, was giving him acting notes during rehearsal. Eric's words were smug and condescending. Whenever he found himself in a situation like this with Eric, he started to fidget. He tried to keep an open mind, but the director's advice was laced with poison. "Ugh," he thought, as cold shivers ran up the arm that Eric had just touched. To make matters worse, Eric's advice wasn't helpful. He talked in a way that reminded Steven of a puffed-up bird. Eric's remarks were always self-congratulatory and he never wasted a chance to refer to his previous accomplishments. Basically, Eric was a blowhard. He wore a ridiculous beret and spoke too slowly, like he was savoring the sound of his own voice. Whenever Eric spoke, Steven found it difficult to concentrate.

As Eric droned on, Steven's frustration increased. His fidgeting turned to agitation. Eric's grandiosity was impossible to tolerate, but Steven was powerless. The rest of the cast was counting on him and he couldn't very well drop the show. They were discussing a scene that made Steven nervous, and Eric's directing style was making things worse. During these encounters, Steven felt horrible about himself while Eric seemed to swell with pride, like his tremendous insights were a gift to everyone in earshot. He wanted to shout in Eric's face. As Eric again found an opportunity to reminisce about past performances, Steven finally lost his patience. "Okay, I get it! I suck and you're brilliant. Why didn't you just cast yourself?!" he exclaimed, and stormed off the stage.

Why Do Narcissists Act This Way?

Sooner or later, most people learn how to let others take center stage every once in a while. From a developmental perspective, accomplishing this milestone is actually a big deal. Young children are notoriously self-centered. It takes years for them to understand that other people have their own thoughts and feelings. It takes even longer before they're able to actively consider other people when making decisions. It's a long road from the self-focused days of early childhood to a selfless stance of genuine compassion. The ability to prioritize others over self is a hallmark of emotional maturity.

Making the leap from egocentrism to emotional maturity is not possible unless children feel secure in their own importance. For the first few years of their lives, growing children need to be the focus of attention. They need to soak up their parents' genuine delight in every little accomplishment and discovery. Like little gold coins that add up over time, a child eventually has a vast store of experiences of when he or she felt important. Another term for this internal store of positive feelings is *narcissistic supply.*

For narcissists, feeling important can be as precious as a last bite of bread to someone stranded on a desert island. When narcissistic supply is low, it is very difficult to let others take the spotlight. The dilemma for narcissists is that their supply is always nearly empty. The storage bins needed to be filled when the person was young, but that

Other Examples of Grandiose Self-Importance

BOASTING OR BRAGGING Narcissists sometimes boast or brag about their accomplishments, whether real or imagined, in an attempt to feel important.

GRANDSTANDING Grandstanding is when a person expresses his opinions in a way that's more about the display than the message. Politicians are often accused of grandstanding when they use a topic to further their own agenda and attract media attention. Everyday examples of grandstanding include talking too loudly about controversial topics in restaurants and public venues, or making posts on social media that are designed to get lots of attention.

BEHAVING LIKE A PRIMA DONNA *Prima donna* is an opera term that originally described the lead singer in a theater company. Today, it means someone who is temperamental and has an inflated view of his or her own talent and importance. Prima donnas never share the spotlight. They make unreasonable demands of others and expect others to gratify and flatter them. Narcissists act like prima donnas when they order food servers around, expect special consideration at social gatherings, or fly into a rage when minor things go wrong. ❯

> CONTINUED

BEING INCONSIDERATE OR INCURIOUS TOWARD OTHERS Narcissists are often inconsiderate of other people. They may take only their own needs and feelings into account, remaining totally oblivious to other people's comfort. In conversation, they may not ask how others are doing or express curiosity about what is happening in other people's lives. They may consistently steer the topic back to themselves and their experiences, even when doing so feels inappropriate to others.

HAVING UNREASONABLY HIGH STANDARDS Grandiose narcissists often have unreasonably high standards for others. When people fail to meet those standards, grandiose narcissists may become critical or even abusive. In contrast, vulnerable narcissists often have unreasonably high standards for themselves. They may consider themselves capable of greatness, fame, or fortune, and may feel depressed and ashamed for not living up to their own unreasonably high standards.

didn't happen. It's not that they want to make others feel less important, it's that they are figuratively starving and need food. Narcissists can't give what they don't have. They are stuck in the search for more narcissistic supply.

Fueling vs. Defusing: Steven's Story

Narcissistic grandiosity is hard to deal with. Sometimes, your instincts might compel you to confront grandiose self-importance with ridicule, anger, or resentment. Unfortunately, those sorts of instincts aren't always helpful. As the old saying goes, two wrongs don't make a right. When you attempt to change someone's negative behavior by treating them negatively, you only escalate an already bad situation. This is especially true when it comes to narcissism, because the person often feels that he or she has done nothing wrong in the first place. Your negative reaction actually reinforces the narcissist's narrative of being a victim. In the case of grandiose narcissists, this will likely result in narcissistic rage or dismissive behavior. Vulnerable narcissists may also respond with rage, but are more likely to become depressed, anxious, or withdrawn.

Another word for this is *fueling* the negative situation. Instead of adding fuel to an already difficult dilemma, it is more helpful to *defuse,* or de-escalate, the situation using your knowledge of narcissism.

Let's take another look at Steven's situation with his director, Eric. Steven's commitment to the show means that he must find a way to tolerate Eric's grandiosity and learn to work together effectively.

Steven's reaction to Eric is partly based on his own feelings of anxiety about being good enough in the role. Eric's behavior toward Steven is amplifying those feelings rather than helping to soothe them. Here is where Steven could communicate more effectively. While he can't change Eric's personality, he can make his own needs known in a way that is nonthreatening to Eric. For example, Steven could say something like, "You know, Eric, I'm actually feeling really nervous about this scene. I'm worried that I'm not going to hit the right emotional chords. I know that you have a lot of experience and I could use some reassurance."

Let's break this down a bit. First, Steven acknowledges how he is feeling. Next, he reassures Eric. He acknowledges Eric's expertise and opens a door for Eric to feel less worried about his own reputation. Finally, Steven asks for what he wants. Notice he doesn't ask for acting advice, because Eric has been giving lots of it and that hasn't been helpful. Steven wants help to feel less anxious. He wants reassurance.

Saying something like this probably goes against Steven's instincts, because it makes Steven more vulnerable in a situation where he already feels insecure. Ironically, Eric is probably feeling the same way underneath his grandiosity. He feels he must constantly mention his past successes because he is secretly insecure about not being good enough. Eric is so preoccupied with his need to maintain his identity as an accomplished performer and director that he is actually unable to see that Steven is the one who needs reassurance.

Remember Narcissus and Echo? Echo couldn't make her feelings known, while Narcissus was too preoccupied with his own reflection to notice. In this example, Steven can't make his feelings known, and Eric is too preoccupied with his reputation to notice. Since Eric is unable to see the effects of his behavior, it is up to Steven to find a way to tell him. If Steven admits that he is nervous and needs reassurance, it can give Eric permission to be less worried about himself and more concerned with helping his actor.

CHAPTER 2

Personal Exceptionalism

Personal exceptionalism is the belief that you are special in a way that sets you above other people. It's the belief that you are more beautiful, wealthy, intelligent, or talented than others, and that this elevated status grants you unique privileges or considerations. In everyday practice, personal exceptionalism is what drives cliques in high school and the workplace, causing groups to bully and exclude those perceived as lower on the social ladder. Personal exceptionalism is also one of the reasons there are special reserved sections in clubs, sporting events, and even airplanes.

Cindy's Story

With Tim, Cindy had "married up." She was raised in a lower-middle class family. While she and her siblings had always had the essentials—enough food, clean clothes, and a stable home—she couldn't remember a time when there hadn't been financial stress. Both of her parents worked full-time throughout Cindy's youth. She and her siblings had been latchkey kids. Later, she had to work and borrow her way through junior college and then a public university.

Tim, on the other hand, came from a much wealthier family. He had attended private university and was debt-free. An only child, he was not accustomed to sharing anything. But it wasn't just Tim's background that distinguished him from Cindy. She loved her career as an elementary school teacher, but often felt like it wasn't good enough for Tim. It simply couldn't compare in terms of pay or prestige to Tim's career as a promising young attorney. A perfectionist with exceedingly high standards for himself and his work, Tim made junior partner at his firm in only five years.

Despite her attempts at self-assurance, Cindy couldn't quite shake the feeling that Tim looked down on her. He would make little disparaging comments about her family and seemed uneasy when they went to her parents' house for holidays. Cindy tried to tell herself that these were just her insecurities and that Tim loved and accepted her for who she was.

In contrast, Tim beamed whenever he spoke about his own family. He seemed to idealize his mother, and he was oddly reverent toward his father. Cindy couldn't understand Tim's relationship with his parents—it felt strangely stilted, like there wasn't any genuine closeness. Although Cindy had made many attempts to get to know Tim's parents, she always came away feeling bad about herself. She never seemed to say the right thing. She had always been funny and outgoing, but had never once made Tim's parents laugh. She felt outmatched when the conversation inevitably turned to politics or art. To make matters worse, Tim seemed to side with his parents in these moments. Cindy felt like an outsider. Whenever she brought this up to Tim, he profusely denied having any idea what she was talking about.

Cindy worried because Tim seemed to be growing increasingly remote. He used to want her by his side at all times, but lately Cindy was left out of business events and parties—even the ones that were supposed to be family-friendly. Meanwhile, Tim had started to talk with unparalleled excitement about being invited to join the same country club as the senior partners at his firm. She was happy for him, but also felt like this new membership just meant more weekends spent alone.

She had no idea how to talk about these worries with Tim. She was tired of feeling looked down upon. She wanted to feel like her husband was proud of her and her career. She wanted to feel like her thoughts and opinions mattered in his world. She wanted Tim to be on her side.

Why Do Narcissists Act This Way?

Many traits and behaviors that people sometimes label narcissistic are perfectly normal—under the right circumstances, they are even accepted. People elevating themselves by excluding others is an unfortunate staple of human social experience. History provides countless examples of people elevating themselves by excluding those they deem inferior. The United States has a long history of using exceptionalist beliefs to justify terrible crimes against marginalized populations. If you search your own history, political beliefs, religious beliefs, and other group affiliations, you may find that you, too, have been guilty of exceptionalism at some point in your life.

Narcissists are forced to define themselves based on the expectations, likes, and dislikes of others. Rather than relying on an internal sense of being good enough, narcissists are stuck seeking approval and reassurance. Without constant infusions of praise and flattery, the false self becomes weak and unstable. The house built over the bottomless pit starts to creak and the floor begins to feel dangerously thin. One way of solving this problem is to gain membership into exclusive groups. By doing so, narcissists can reassure themselves that they are good enough because they are doing better than others.

I once knew a person who would say, "I wonder what the poor people are doing tonight?" as a way of reassuring himself that he was a financial success. Perhaps this was because he didn't have strong values of his own.

Other Examples of Personal Exceptionalism

NAME-DROPPING This is the practice of casually inserting information into a conversation with the intention of impressing others. Name-dropping can include important people that the person knows (or claims to know), exotic destinations to which the person has traveled, expensive brands or labels that the person owns, or other information that is meant to convey elevated status. Narcissists often name-drop at parties or other social gatherings (including social media) to make themselves appear important and special.

ACTING ABOVE THE RULES Things work best when everyone plays by the same rules. Sometimes narcissists who exhibit the trait of personal exceptionalism behave as though they are not subject to the same rules as everyone else. They may only obey rules when it suits them, making exceptions when they want something that the rules prohibit. They may convince themselves that it is okay to cheat, steal, or lie. They may drive over the speed limit because they think they are better drivers than everyone else. They may have one set of rules for themselves, and an entirely different set of rules for others—often with little to no sense of personal hypocrisy.

ALWAYS BEING RIGHT It's hard to admit being wrong. Nobody likes to accept defeat. It can be embarrassing and uncomfortable. Nevertheless, most people know that they can't always be right. Grandiose narcissists, on the other hand, can be so defended against feelings of shame and humiliation that they convince themselves they are always right. Even when their errors are pointed out to them, they may engage in complicated rationalizations to avoid admitting they were wrong. They may also blame others for their own mistakes, genuinely believing that they were in the right the whole time. This is called externalizing. Vulnerable narcissists often have the unconscious belief that they *should* always be right. This belief triggers feelings of shame and depression when they make mistakes.

BEING ASHAMED OF OTHERS Healthy emotional boundaries allow people to separate their own actions from the actions of others. Most people understand that somebody else's less attractive qualities have no bearing on their own worth. Narcissists are not always able to make such distinctions. For example, they may feel ashamed or embarrassed to be seen with someone they find unattractive. Similarly, they may feel humiliated if a friend makes a mistake, or if a romantic partner isn't looking his or her best on a given day. These poor emotional boundaries typically cause the narcissist to engage in controlling or avoiding behaviors in an attempt to avoid embarrassment.

Instead, he relied on external markers of success, such as perceived membership in an exclusive class of people who are financially well-off. For this person, being good enough meant being better than someone else. His success was defined by other people's failures.

Some narcissists rely very heavily on this tactic to reinforce a fragile sense of self. They seek entry into exclusive clubs, restaurants, and venues. They will only fly first class and wear designer brands. They pride themselves on possessing exclusive information or knowing important people. By doing these things, narcissists seek to compare themselves favorably to others. This sense of "being better off" is used to replenish narcissistic supply.

Fueling vs. Defusing: Cindy's Story

Cindy's situation with Tim is a good example of narcissism passing from one generation to the next, known as intergenerational transmission. Intergenerational transmission can happen with almost any personality trait or mental health issue. Depression, anxiety, trauma, and substance abuse can all be passed from parents to children. Tim's parents have narcissistic traits that have been passed down to Tim, who has learned to identify with his parents (i.e., act just like them) to avoid feeling the way that Cindy does when she spends time with them.

As you may recall, Cindy typically feels bad about herself after spending an evening with Tim's parents. Whereas she normally gets along well with others, Tim's parents make her feel inadequate, alienated, and incompetent. They do this in subtle ways, such as not laughing at her jokes (which makes her feel uncomfortable and foolish) and discussing topics that they know a lot about but Cindy does not. These are not the behaviors of gracious hosts. Rather, they are ways of making themselves feel special and privileged at Cindy's expense. These behaviors also make Tim feel conflict about his choice of a partner. While Cindy feels the need to impress Tim's parents at dinner, Tim has felt that way his whole life. He unconsciously sides with his parents when they make Cindy feel foolish because he learned at an early age that not siding with them meant becoming a target himself. Without realizing it, Tim acts out this relationship pattern in other places as well. At work, he idealizes the senior partners and longs to be accepted by them. He also longs for inclusion in exclusive clubs and venues because gaining such memberships makes Tim feel like he is good enough.

Cindy is caught between two generations of narcissists. While she may not be able to do much with respect to Tim's parents, she can work to make Tim more aware of her feelings. Like Steven in the previous chapter, Cindy must make herself vulnerable. Tim is terrified of not belonging because he grew up feeling the constant threat of his parents' disappointment. For him, these feelings aren't simply the result of an uncomfortable evening—they have built up over a lifetime. He is unconsciously placing Cindy in the same predicament as the one in which he was raised. Cindy can help Tim become more aware by owning her feelings of inadequacy and alienation. She must be able to give voice to the feelings that Tim is too afraid to see in himself.

Rather than join Tim in his lifelong quest to feel accepted, Cindy can instead tell Tim just how much it hurts to feel different and left out. She can express the truth of her feelings without needing Tim to vilify his parents. She might say something like, "Did you know that I often end up feeling unimportant and bad about myself after we visit your parents? Have you ever felt that way?" Rather than accuse Tim of siding with his parents and leaving her out of work functions, Cindy can express her desire to be by his side. She could say, "I'm so proud of you and your success. I would really like to be able to stand by your side and support you at your work functions." This will make Tim feel wanted, instead of accused of being a bad husband. Finally, instead of trying to compensate for the feelings of inadequacy that Tim's parents cause her to feel, she can connect with her own sense of worth and goodness—something that neither of Tim's parents are able to do on their own. This makes Cindy more powerful than either of them, and it's a model for Tim to follow.

CHAPTER 3

Arrogant, Haughty Behaviors and Attitudes

The word *haughty* is defined as "blatantly and disdainfully proud." Arrogant, haughty behavior is like a combination of grandiose self-importance and personal exceptionalism, with a dash of condescension. It's not just the belief that you are better or more important than others; you also believe that others are inferior. If you've ever been talked down to, had your opinion intentionally minimized or discounted, or otherwise been made to feel inferior, then you've experienced this trait in action.

Stephanie's Story

Stephanie's wife, Jamie, was 20 years her senior. The two had been married for three years, two of which had been amazing. For the most part, Stephanie felt safe with Jamie, who was financially established and even had a grown son of her own. She also looked up to Jamie. She valued her advice and respected her opinion.

Before meeting Jamie, Stephanie had lived a tumultuous life. Now, in the last three years, Stephanie had started going to Alcoholics Anonymous (AA) meetings again, had been hired as an administrative assistant at a local firm, and was even thinking about going back to school. All of it was due to Jamie's encouragement and support.

But Jamie's support had a sharp edge. She could be fantastically positive and encouraging, but she could also be critical and condescending—even a little mean. She criticized Stephanie for not keeping the house clean, for not dressing better, and for maintaining friendships with people who didn't meet Jamie's approval. She called them "garbage people." Some nights, when Stephanie was getting ready to go out with these friends, Jamie would grumble, "I guess you want to stay a garbage person."

In Stephanie's eyes, Jamie seemed perfect. She was always put together and always knew the right answers. Compared to Jamie, Stephanie often did feel like a "garbage person." She felt ashamed of her past and insecure about her ability to make good choices. Sometimes, she wondered if she relied too heavily on

Jamie's opinion. She always made sure to check in with Jamie before making decisions. Even so, Jamie would still make it seem like it was Stephanie's fault if things didn't turn out well.

Stephanie doubted the validity of her feelings. She wanted to feel respected by her spouse, but perhaps Jamie was right. Perhaps she didn't deserve to be respected until she could make better decisions and take better care of herself. Perhaps she would always be a "garbage person."

Why Do Narcissists Act This Way?

Arrogance or haughtiness is a way to get rid of feelings of inferiority and shame by offloading them onto others. Imagine a game of "hot potato": The object of the game is to not be the one stuck holding the potato when time runs out. You get rid of the potato by throwing it to someone else, making it that person's problem instead. For narcissists, feeling inferior or ashamed is like holding a hot potato. All they want to do is get rid of it. One way of doing this is to throw the hot potato to someone else. Another way to describe this is *scapegoating*, or the act of singling someone out and shifting blame or punishment to them.

The word *scapegoat* refers to an ancient religious practice in which a community's sins would be symbolically laid upon a goat, which was then sent out into the wilderness to die. This allowed the community to ritualistically rid itself of unwanted qualities and avoid punishment. The goat was made to suffer as a stand-in for the people. In today's world, scapegoating can include blaming someone else for your own mistakes or taking the heat off yourself by making someone else feel stupid, foolish, or ridiculous.

Narcissists adopt attitudes of superiority while thumbing their noses at those they identify as inferior. This allows them to feel safe from the insecurities they have symbolically expelled, much in the same way scapegoating helped ancient people feel safe from punishment.

Like the other traits discussed in Part 1, this offloading of bad feelings is not done consciously. Most narcissists would not admit that they are, in effect, punishing others for their own sins. In fact, most narcissists would not even be willing to admit that their actions have any negative effect on others. As mentioned earlier, grandiose traits of narcissism rely on two primary psychological defenses: denial and projection.

Fueling vs. Defusing: Stephanie's Story

Narcissism is sometimes associated with the positive personality traits of leadership and authority—qualities that Stephanie needed to help her get her life together. With Jamie's support, Stephanie was able to contain self-doubt and focus her energy in a more productive direction. Nevertheless, Jamie's arrogance and haughty attitude began to eat away at the very confidence that Stephanie is trying to build.

Other Examples of Arrogance and Haughtiness

BULLYING BEHAVIOR Whether in the schoolyard or the corporate boardroom, bullying involves elevating oneself at the expense of others. The victim is often made to feel inferior and unsafe, while the bully uses intimidation to feel powerful. Grandiose narcissists often bully people in overt ways such as name-calling, mocking or ridiculing appearance, or taking advantage of vulnerabilities in others to make themselves look better. Vulnerable narcissists tend to use less direct methods of bullying, such as emotional coercion or passive aggression. For example, vulnerable narcissists may make others feel obligated to give them compliments or make loved ones feel pressured to devote excessive amounts of time, energy, and emotional resources to the narcissist.

HIGH-HANDED BEHAVIOR This term describes disregard for the thoughts, feelings, or rights of others. Marie Antoinette's infamous remark, "Let them eat cake!" is a fine example of high-handedness. Upon hearing that peasants didn't have bread, she allegedly suggested that they eat cake instead (which was considerably more expensive and difficult to obtain than bread), demonstrating the extent of her ignorance and apathy toward the plight ›

> CONTINUED

of her subjects. Narcissists behave in a high-handed manner when they don't treat their friends, spouses, or coworkers as equals, and instead order them about in arrogant or dismissive ways.

DISMISSIVE BEHAVIOR Recent research comparing narcissism to attachment styles (i.e., the characteristic ways that people behave in relationships) suggests that grandiose narcissism is associated with a dismissive-avoidant attachment style. In other words, grandiose narcissists typically avoid emotional intimacy and behave in dismissive ways toward people they care about. They may claim not to have enough time for loved ones, or they may appear distracted or preoccupied when they should be listening and actively engaging. Such dismissive behavior is motivated by the inability to empathize with the other person's feelings, or by the belief that other people's problems aren't as important as the narcissist's own concerns.

JUDGMENTAL BEHAVIOR Everyone is judgmental from time to time. Forming judgments is one of the mind's primary means of protection. If it weren't for the ability to form snap judgments about unfamiliar people and situations, humanity's story would have ended as a sinewy meal for some lucky ancient predator. But if you aren't careful, you can get trapped in the mind's own system of categorizing and judging. It can be easy to forget that good and bad are mental constructs that never tell the whole story, leaving you stuck trying to be "good," "worthy," or "special" to avoid being "bad." When the mind's judgments go unquestioned, a lot of people end up judging everything and everyone, including themselves. This is both the cause and end result of judgmental behavior in narcissism. In grandiose narcissists, arrogance or haughtiness is based on an internal battle between judgments. To avoid being "bad," the narcissist must be "good." To stay "good," the narcissist must label others as "bad." For vulnerable narcissists, the situation is inverted. Vulnerable narcissists often feel like the "bad" ones and have the impression that everyone else is "good."

This is a common relationship configuration. Narcissists often partner with those down on their luck. They thrive on the feeling of being important and needed, so you can see how someone like Jamie might be attracted to Stephanie. That's not to say that their entire relationship is based on Stephanie having been a hard luck case. Rather, Stephanie's need for a surrogate parent and Jamie's desire to be needed provide an emotional context, or a way that their relationship makes unconscious sense to each of them. Another term for this is *unconscious partner choice*. If you've ever heard someone complain that they are always attracted to the wrong type of person, then you've heard the results of unconscious partner choice.

The unconscious partner choice between Stephanie and Jamie has a built-in time limit unless they work together to create a different basis for their relationship. If they don't, Stephanie will eventually outgrow her need for Jamie's parental role. Stephanie will feel resentful of Jamie's attempts to control her, and Jamie will feel frustrated because she is no longer needed. Their relationship has already begun to transform in this direction. In response to Stephanie's growing independence, Jamie has started to criticize her in an unconscious attempt to keep her dependent. Without intervention, their relationship will quickly become toxic.

One of the most immediate threats to the relationship is Jamie's growing criticism of Stephanie, who reacts with a mix of self-doubt ("maybe I am a garbage person") and defiance. As with the other stories in Part 1, it is up to Stephanie to take a step into her own feelings of vulnerability and inadequacy if she wants Jamie to understand how she feels.

To accomplish this, Stephanie can try a technique sometimes used by therapists to keep sessions from becoming too heated. It involves addressing the intention behind what a person is saying rather than the content (another word for this is *process*). When Jamie makes a critical remark, Stephanie could respond by saying something like, "I just heard you say _____ and it made me feel really bad about myself. Is that what you intended?" Notice that Stephanie's comment is not an accusation. No blame or malice is implied. Instead, she is stating her feelings and following up with a question. This allows Stephanie a chance to take responsibility for her emotions while helping Jamie to be more conscious of her own actions and intentions. If Jamie responds with another criticism, Stephanie can maintain her nonthreatening and reflective stance by saying something like, "I just heard you say _____. How do you think that makes me feel?" This can be continued indefinitely, always following the same basic format.

If Stephanie allows herself to respond to the content of Jamie's criticism (e.g., whether or not Stephanie and her friends are garbage), the conversation will only end with both of them feeling angry and frustrated. If she instead keeps a process-oriented focus, then she never needs to defend herself or her friends. She can simply repeat back Jamie's critical remarks, acknowledge how they made her feel, and ask if that was what Jamie intended.

In the next chapter, we'll learn about a few more ways to deal with grandiose behavior, as well as some suggestions for healing techniques.

CHAPTER 4

Dealing with Grandiose Behavior

The key to dealing with grandiose behavior is to understand that narcissists use it to cope with deep feelings of insecurity. At some point in their development, narcissists were made to feel like their true thoughts and feelings didn't matter. They were used as a mirror—their sole purpose was to reflect a flattering image. They are loath to reexperience those feelings of being used. Grandiosity protects them from feeling vulnerable. For vulnerable narcissists, grandiosity remains disguised beneath more visible symptoms.

The problem with narcissistic grandiosity is that it causes other people to feel the feelings that the narcissist is trying to expel. Grandiose narcissists make others feel inferior and unimportant by acting superior, while vulnerable narcissists make others feel inferior and unimportant because they are too preoccupied with their own self-esteem to really see and care for those around them. Both types of narcissists unconsciously use others in the same way that they were used as children.

Respond Instead of React

Grandiose behavior can be incredibly difficult to tolerate. If someone is actively talking down to you, turning their nose up at you, criticizing you, or excluding you, your first instinct is probably to find some way of firing back. Resist this temptation. The only effective way to deal with grandiosity is to avoid joining the narcissist in the game of emotional hot potato. The narcissist is unconsciously attempting to off-load bad feelings onto you. If you try to throw them back, you will only perpetuate a pattern that feels bad for everyone involved. Besides, the narcissist is much better at playing this game; she has been doing it for years.

The key to dealing with grandiosity is to *respond* instead of *react*. Reacting is usually more of a reflex than a deliberate choice. The results are unpredictable and often not very helpful. When you respond, you give yourself space to take in what is happening and choose the best way to proceed. Narcissists are incapable of responding to feelings of insecurity in a thoughtful and balanced manner because such feelings threaten to destabilize their false self. Your task is to do what the narcissist cannot.

Take a chance and step into your own vulnerability. Allow yourself to feel the bad feelings that the narcissist's grandiose behavior is triggering in you. If you are able to hold these feelings and not react to them, you will be able to see that they really belong to the narcissist. You've been given the narcissists feelings of not being good, important, or lovable. By giving you these bad feelings, the narcissist is actually communicating something that he could never explicitly say. Once you've seen this, you can make a choice about how to respond. Perhaps you say nothing. Perhaps you gently change the subject. Or, perhaps you give voice to these feelings—feelings that you can hold, but the narcissist can't. When you admit to feeling anxious, insecure, or unimportant, it gives the narcissist permission to feel the same way. Will this work for every narcissist? Nope. You can't control anyone's behavior but your own. While taking this approach probably won't work right away—and it definitely won't work every time—it will give you the peace of mind of knowing that you are responding in an ethical, mindful, and compassionate manner.

Here are a few tips for dealing with grandiosity in specific types of relationships.

Partner or Ex-Partner

Grandiosity from a romantic partner or ex-partner is particularly difficult because people tend to think of their partners as equals. Although marriages used to feature significant power differences between husbands and wives, modern unions are more often a 50–50 partnership. Even if you aren't married, odds are you expect your romantic partner to treat you as a peer, not as a subordinate.

When a romantic partner behaves in a grandiose manner, it can build resentment. Allowing yourself to be vulnerable and express your feelings rather than clam up or lash out can feel especially risky.

Try approaching your partner or ex-partner when the stakes are low and both of you are calm. Have an idea of what you'd like to say beforehand. Express your feeling that sometimes they act in a way that makes you feel unimportant. Let them know that you don't think they intend to do it, but that it happens anyway. Give a few concrete examples (again, it helps to prepare ahead of time). Say something like, "I don't want to argue or fight about this right now. I just wanted you to know how I feel."

Parent

Parents get used to being in charge of their children. Sometimes, old habits die hard when kids grow up and want to redefine the relationship. It's important to remember that grandiosity is a cover for insecurity. Perhaps your parent is worried that she didn't do a very good job, or wonders what her purpose is now that you're grown. Perhaps she wants to feel needed, important, or respected. If you can find the insecurity, then you can short-circuit the grandiosity by speaking to insecurity instead.

Try waiting until the stakes are low and you are both calm before having a talk. Let your parent know how appreciative you are and how much you want the relationship to improve. Describe the problematic behavior and talk about how that specific behavior makes you feel less important, invisible, or like your opinions don't matter. If your parent responds defensively, try gently shifting gears to address whatever insecurity you feel might be hidden under the grandiosity. Say something like, "I feel like you might be concerned about _____ and I want you to know that _____."

Boss or Coworker

Grandiosity in the workplace represents a unique challenge because tense or contentious relationships with bosses and coworkers can result in job loss. Moreover, not every work environment is conducive to discussing relationship dynamics. Sometimes shifting your own perspective is the most effective way to manage the effects of another person's grandiosity. This may seem like you're dodging the issue, but learning not to make things worse can actually be a huge improvement. Once you are aware that grandiose behavior is the narcissist's way of trying to throw a negative "hot potato" to you, you can simply refuse to play. This might mean ignoring the behavior or neutrally changing the subject.

If the person is in a position of authority, one option might be to use the narcissist's own grandiosity in your favor by strategically going along with it. As a therapy technique, this is called *rolling with the resistance*. Rather than struggling against the tide, you go along with it and gradually work your way into a better position. Note that

When a Narcissist Also Has Antisocial Personality Traits

Antisocial personality disorder is basically the modern term for psychopathy. People with this disorder are deceitful and aggressive, have low empathy, and lack remorse for their actions. Typically, people with antisocial traits see vulnerability as a weakness to exploit. Narcissism and antisocial personality disorder can sometimes mix together in the same person. This is called malignant narcissism. People like this can be dangerous. If the behavior of the narcissistic person in your life feels sadistic (i.e., they enjoy when others are in pain) or if you have witnessed the person knowingly hurting, abusing, or taking advantage of others, you may be dealing with a malignant narcissist. The relationship is likely not salvageable. If you are being abused or the relationship is unsafe, the most important priorities are your personal and emotional safety. Seek help and support from family, friends, and trained professionals.

using this technique doesn't mean you have to become a suck-up. You don't have to sacrifice your integrity to say something like, "It sounds like you feel really great about this project," or "I agree that you have done a lot for this company." Of course, if a boss's or coworker's grandiose behavior is abusive, then it may be time to think about escalating the situation using the options available at your place of work. These options include contacting your human resources department, speaking with your union rep, or even asking for a mediated face-to-face meeting with the problematic individual.

Healing Techniques

Techniques for healing and reflection appear throughout this book. Of course, none of the advice in this book is intended to be a "magic bullet" to cure your problems with the narcissists in your life. Sadly, there's no such thing, and anyone claiming otherwise is being dishonest. What this book *can* offer are suggestions that, with time and steady effort, add up to big changes in your life and relationships.

Mindfulness Meditation

Mindfulness meditation is a well-researched and effective method for reducing stress, depression, and anxiety and increasing overall well-being. It's simple and takes as little as five minutes per day to start.

The goal of mindfulness meditation is to adopt a posture of nonjudgmental present-moment awareness. Issues like depression, stress, and anxiety tend to become worse when people spend time dwelling on past events and imagining what could happen in the future. They are also made worse when the mind engages in unchecked judgments about self, others, and situations beyond immediate control. Mindfulness meditation is basically a way to practice continually returning your attention to the moment at hand.

Here's what to do: First, find a comfortable place to sit and set a timer for five minutes. Many people sit cross-legged on the floor, using a small cushion as a seat. Keep a straight back and let your hands rest gently and comfortably in your lap. Close your eyes, or let your gaze fall softly on the floor just in front of you. Now, observe your breathing. Breathe in and out through your nose, letting your attention fall on the spot where the breath enters and leaves your body. Notice the sensations there. Feel the coolness of it, the slight tingling sensation. Allow your attention to rest in that sensation as you breathe normally.

You'll notice your mind wandering. Memories, plans, judgments, and other sensations will dance across your awareness. At first, it may seem like an avalanche of thoughts. When you notice that your mind has strayed from your breathing, gently acknowledge your thoughts. Then, bring your attention back to that place where the breath is going in and out. You may do this dozens of times in your first few sittings.

When five minutes is up, simply get up and go about your day. That's it! That's literally all there is to it. Just be forewarned that it's easier said than done. Mindfulness meditation is a way to practice simply observing the mind rather than getting dragged around by every thought or feeling you have. As you get more comfortable, try increasing your meditation time from five to ten minutes. After a few weeks, try fifteen or twenty minutes. Eventually, you may even be able to sit for thirty or forty minutes. With daily practice, you will likely find yourself feeling less stressed and more centered.

Exploring Vulnerability

As discussed, narcissists use grandiosity to get rid of bad feelings and avoid vulnerability. It's impossible to improve your relationship with the narcissist in your life by joining them in trying to flee from vulnerable feelings like shame, inadequacy, and sadness. This exercise is designed to help you get better acquainted with your own vulnerable feelings and to increase your ability to be with them.

First, make a list of the negative thoughts and feelings you have about yourself. Ideally, they should be thoughts and feelings that are connected to the narcissist in your life. Try not to dwell on each thing that you write down. Instead, just acknowledge that everyone has insecurities and these are yours. Cap the list at around five things.

Next, make a small pile of flashcards based on these insecurities. Find a comfortable place to sit and go through the cards one by one. Try to really connect with the feeling or thought on each card. If it hurts, let it hurt. If there's fear, allow yourself to feel it. If there's sadness or anger, acknowledge it and let it stay for a little while. Let each feeling come in and sit with it for a minute, like you are inviting it to share a cup of tea. The feeling is just a guest; it won't stay forever. While it's here, try to get to know it a bit.

When you are ready, close your eyes and focus on your breathing. Take a few cleansing breaths before opening your eyes and moving to the next card. If it gets too intense or too tiring, take a break.

Afterward, reflect on the feelings you explored. Notice how they started off small, rose to peak intensity, and then went away. This is the nature of all feelings. They never stick around, not even the good ones. Once you're better acquainted with each feeling, think about it in terms of the hot potato game discussed earlier. You can use these feelings to understand what the narcissist is feeling. Each one represents something that the narcissist is trying to get rid of or is afraid to feel. When these feelings come up again in your relationship, you can use this information to gain insight into the narcissist's grandiose behavior. This practice allows you to feel empathy and compassion, rather than anger or disgust, and allows you to *respond* to grandiosity rather than *react* to it.

PART

2

The Self-Serving Dimension

While grandiosity protects the narcissist from feelings of inadequacy and shame, self-serving traits protect the narcissist from feeling depleted, empty, and abandoned. All narcissists, whether grandiose or vulnerable, are self-centered. For both groups, the self-centeredness derives from an inner state of emergency.

Beneath their arrogant and controlling exterior, grandiose narcissists are full of fear, shame, and self-loathing. To avoid these internal reservoirs of pain, grandiose narcissists work tirelessly to maintain a façade of perfection. The façade must be convincing to everyone involved— most importantly, it must convince the narcissist. Any cracks in this perfect exterior threaten to destabilize the narcissist and send her tumbling into insecurity. This existential issue keeps grandiose narcissists focused on themselves.

Unconsciously, grandiose narcissists are in crisis and simply trying to survive. Most have no conscious awareness of this desperation and inner pain. They protect themselves with feelings of superiority and blamelessness. Even when victimizing or exploiting others, they cast themselves as heroes of the story. Rather than experience their raw hunger for acceptance, love, and attention, grandiose narcissists substitute a sense that they deserve the resources they crave. They tell themselves that they need praise and admiration because they deserve it, not because their sense of self will collapse without it. They justify minimizing your feelings because they have so much on their plate right now, not because they struggle with basic empathy. They rationalize taking advantage of your generosity because they have done so much for you, not because they are in a perpetual state of taking from others.

When any of these defenses are pointed out, grandiose narcissists tend to respond with anger and blame. Another term for this is *narcissistic rage*. The severity of this rage is testament to the desperation that lurks beneath. Like cornered animals in fear for their survival, grandiose narcissists often lash out ferociously when their defenses are questioned.

Vulnerable narcissists, too, feel starved for self-esteem resources. Unlike their grandiose counterparts, vulnerable narcissists don't have a conscious narrative of superiority to justify and rationalize their self-centered treatment of others. Instead, they tend to minimize just how much emotional space they actually occupy. In fact, most vulnerable narcissists feel chronically invisible, overlooked, underappreciated, or unwanted. Although they may be asking for an incredible amount of emotional resources from friends, family, or romantic partners, they often feel that they hardly ask for anything at all. From their perspective, they keep a lot to themselves.

Vulnerable narcissists are often acutely aware of their dependency on others. They feel lonely, isolated, and unloved. They are terrified of telling others that they feel disappointed or angry because they imagine it will lead to rejection and abandonment. Instead, they hold these thoughts and feelings inside, which only increases feelings of invisibility. When they finally work up the courage to express what has been welling up inside of them, it often comes out in an uneven and blaming way. This, in turn, causes misunderstandings and more feelings of invisibility. The cycle continues.

In short, narcissists are not good at considering others. Their self-focus and excessive demands often occupy too much space. The next few chapters will look closely at the traits that occupy narcissism's self-serving dimension, as well as ways of dealing with them.

CHAPTER 5

A Strong Sense of Entitlement

Entitlement is a central feature of narcissism. It means feeling that you have a right to something, regardless of whether or not you've earned it. People can feel entitled to money, time, attention, sex, special treatment, or anything else perceived to have value.

Entitlement comes in different forms. Sometimes, it's specific to a particular relationship, place, or situation, such as feeling entitled to a pay raise or a price discount at the store. It can also be reflected in a person's general attitude or demeanor, such as when someone takes up too much of your time, puts their feet on your coffee table, or puts their bag down on the empty seat next to them during rush hour on the subway.

Diane's Story

Michelle and Diane were often paired for projects at work. Although they were supposed to work as a team, Michelle would conveniently neglect to return phone calls or would disappear for off-site meetings. When the finished product was due, Michelle would take an equal share of the credit for less than an equal share of the work. Diane's attempts to address this issue with Michelle never seemed to go anywhere. Diane always ended up feeling like she was being petty or overreacting.

Once again, Michelle was trying to weasel her way out of doing her share. She'd had the gall to ask if Diane would "do her a favor" and "cover for her" while she went on a vacation with her boyfriend the following week. Diane knew that she would end up doing the remainder of the work on their project while Michelle was off having fun.

For the most part, Diane actually liked Michelle. She was energetic, boisterous, and funny. But despite Michelle's positive qualities, Diane was growing increasingly frustrated with their relationship. Michelle took up a lot of space. She talked a little too loudly, gestured a little too fervently, and dressed a little too audaciously. She had an annoying habit of walking uninvited into Diane's workspace and sitting on Diane's desk. Michelle also spent a lot of time talking about herself. She seldom asked questions about Diane, and frequently interrupted Diane when she was speaking.

Diane and Michelle used to spend time together outside work, but Michelle was often late and had a tendency to cancel plans at the last minute. She seldom apologized or even acknowledged these behaviors, leaving Diane feeling frustrated and unimportant. When they did manage to get together for dinner or drinks, Michelle would order expensive items and pressure Diane into splitting the check down the middle.

Diane felt stuck. She wanted to maintain a positive working relationship with Michelle, but was tired of being taken for granted. She considered speaking to management, but worried that this would sour the relationship and make her work environment uncomfortable.

Why Do Narcissists Act This Way?

Entitlement isn't always a negative thing. As society becomes more global, people are becoming increasingly mindful of ethical mandates that everyone, regardless of race, creed, or socioeconomic status, is entitled to things like clean water, enough food to eat, and basic sanitation. Many countries have entitlements enshrined in their constitutions. One such example is the United States' Bill of Rights—a list of things to which every citizen is entitled.

When you're young, you should also be entitled to your parents' love. Nobody asked to be born. People come into this world having no concept of who or what they are. Young people need to be shown their intrinsic value in loving and patient ways. Young people need to be shown over and over again that they are entitled to parental love and positive regard, just as any citizen of the United States is entitled to freedom of speech.

Parental love should be constant and unconditional. It shouldn't be withdrawn because a child didn't follow directions or because mom or dad had a bad day at work, nor should it be contingent upon getting good grades, being polite, or behaving in church. Conditional love creates a dilemma for growing children. They become insecure and worried about how to "earn" the love and positive regard to which they should simply be entitled. This brings about a dependency dilemma, in which their age-appropriate and healthy feelings of dependency (e.g., needs for love, attachment, reassurance) become cause for anxiety and frustration. They attempt to protect themselves from these painful emotions through self-sufficiency.

To ask for things is a form of dependency because it makes you vulnerable to people saying *no*. It is far safer to simply expect things and become angry when they don't magically appear. This places the deficiency with the other person, who failed to live up to your expectations. Instead of being a small, frightened, *dependent* person, you are transformed into a strong, self-assured, *independent* person. You never have to worry about not having enough, because you are entitled to as much as you want.

Other Examples of Entitlement

FEELING PUT UPON Narcissists are hyper-focused on having enough for themselves. They often feel like others ask too much or are inconsiderate of their needs. Even though they actually place excessive demands on others, narcissists have a tendency to feel chronically put upon or overburdened. They often use a narrative of victimhood to justify their entitled behavior.

SELF-ABSORPTION Entitlement can take the form of self-absorption, or feeling preoccupied with one's own needs and feelings. Remember the house built over the bottomless pit? Narcissists spend a lot of time worrying and fussing over the house to make sure it won't collapse. The self-absorption is born of fear, not pride. However, after it is filtered through the narcissist's internal defenses against feeling afraid, the end result may look like pride.

A psychologist named Abraham Maslow theorized that every person has a hierarchy of needs. At the bottom of the hierarchy are things that are essential to staying alive, such as basic safety and having enough to eat. At the top are more abstract concepts, such as self-esteem and self-actualization. Maslow's idea was that you can't worry about the higher order needs until you've taken care of the more basic ones. Narcissists are preoccupied with having a functional, stable sense of self. This is a basic need for them, and it keeps them focused on themselves. Just as you wouldn't worry about making art if you hadn't eaten in days, narcissists are self-absorbed because they feel their psychological survival is in danger.

FREELOADING Narcissists may take advantage of other people's kindness and generosity by freeloading. They may overstay their welcome, take more than their fair share, or make others feel obligated to give them more than they need or deserve. Common examples of free-loading include things like filling one's pockets with free samples, illegal downloading, pressuring friends and family into hosting events or paying for meals, or riding other people's coattails in the workplace.

MAKING PERSONAL EXCEPTIONS This trait overlaps with personal exceptionalism described earlier. Narcissists often feel that they don't need to obey the same rules or laws as everyone else. Sometimes this is based on the belief that they are better than others, but it can also originate out of a sense of entitlement. For example, some people habitually drive over the speed limit because they feel they are better drivers than everyone else (personal exception-alism), while others may do so because they prioritize their urgency over other people's safety (entitlement).

As with other narcissistic traits, entitlement looks different for grandiose and vulnerable narcissists. For grandiose narcissists, entitlement is often about having the best of something (as Gaston menacingly says in the beginning of *Beauty and the Beast*, "Don't I deserve the best?") or receiving special consideration (e.g., VIP treatment at a club or restaurant). For vulnerable narcissists, entitlement is often implicit (under the surface). Vulnerable narcissists expect others to admire them and be impressed by their accomplishments. When this doesn't happen, they treat it as a failure on their part or an indication that others don't like them. Rather than *acting out* by raging at others, they *act in* by becoming angry with themselves.

Fueling vs. Defusing: Diane's Story

Diane's situation is difficult, both because she is dealing with a coworker, and because Michelle's entitlement is subtle. Michelle uses her vivacious personality and superficial charm to freeload off Diane's hard work. Her personal intrusiveness, chronic lateness, and last-minute cancelling of social plans are a testament to her overall lack of consideration for other people.

When Diane brought up her feelings in the past, she was tentative and unsure. Whether or not it's conscious, Michelle is taking advantage of Diane's discomfort with confrontation and her desire to be liked. If Diane wants to feel better about her relationship with Michelle, she needs to set some boundaries.

Dealing with self-serving traits like entitlement is all about setting boundaries. People need boundaries to be healthy and happy. If you removed all the doors from your home and opened all the windows, in a matter of days your house would be unlivable. Wild animals, insects, garbage, and squatters would all begin to settle in your home, and you would have a difficult time getting them out. Even if you succeeded, what would keep them from coming right back in?

As much as people need boundaries to protect their selves and possessions, the same applies to time, energy, personal space, and emotional and psychological space. You need to be able to tell people *no*, or you will not have enough for yourself, much less your loved ones.

Diane's apprehensions about rocking the boat and making things uncomfortable at work are understandable. Then again, maintaining the status quo and being taken advantage of by Michelle will do nothing to make things better. In fact, it will only push this problem down the line to a future date, when Diane will have to deal with it all over again. To take care of herself, she needs to do something different from what she has done in the past.

Diane's best move in this situation is to simply tell Michelle that she can't cover for her while she goes on vacation. She doesn't need to be harsh or mean. For instance, Diane could say, "I know you were probably hoping I'd be able to cover for you, and it sounds like a really great trip, but I won't be able to do it this time. Maybe you guys could postpone your trip for a few weeks until our project is done." Michelle may have a negative reaction or try to escalate the situation in some way (e.g., guilt-tripping, pleading, flattering, throwing a tantrum). If she does, Diane can simply remain neutral and repeat "I know. I'm sorry but I just can't do it." If Michelle asks for reasons, Diane could either respond that she "has a lot going on right now in her life," or she could own her actual feelings and say something like "I'm just not comfortable taking on that much." If Diane sticks to her guns and doesn't give in to Michelle's entitled requests, then Michelle will likely stop making them in the future.

Just as doors and windows keep unwanted things out of our homes, relationship boundaries keep unwanted behaviors out of our lives. The next chapter delves into a second trait of narcissism's self-serving dimension: a lack of empathy.

CHAPTER 6

Lacks Empathy

Although empathy and sympathy are often used inter-changeably, they are actually very different. Sympathy is when you feel sorry for someone. You can see that the person is having a difficult time, and you wish things could be different. You might offer your sympathies when someone loses a loved one, for instance. It's a way of saying "I understand that times are tough and I feel bad for you." Empathy, on the other hand, goes beyond just feeling sorry for someone. It involves imagining what it's like to be that person and to see the world from his perspective. Empathy is when you place yourself in someone else's shoes.

Another way of drawing this distinction is to say that sympathy is something you feel about a person, while empathy is something you feel *as though you were that person.* To use an example from a familiar context, when you watch a play, you *sympathize* with the characters on stage. The actors, though, *empathize* with the characters they are playing.

Narcissists struggle with empathy. They are so consumed with their own needs and concerns that they find it impossible to imagine what it's like to be anyone else. Sometimes, low empathy takes the form of actively cold and insensitive behavior, such as dismissing someone's hurt feelings as unimportant. It can also take the form of passively insensitive behavior, such as failing to notice the needs and feelings of others due to inattention or self-focus.

Jake's Story

Jake was going through a difficult time. He was laid off due to job cuts five months ago. At first, he tried to be optimistic. In addition to job hunting, he used his free time to make some improvements around the house and go to the gym more often. He even took up gardening in the backyard. Now, five months later, he was still unemployed. He couldn't afford to keep making home improvements, and winter had put the gardening on hold. He'd begun to sink into depression. He'd even started taking antidepressants and going to therapy.

In the last few months, Jake had gained almost twenty pounds. Although he spent most of his time in bed, he had trouble sleeping. He simply didn't feel motivated to do much of anything. Feeling this way was hard enough, but what made things really difficult was the growing impatience and insensitivity of his wife, Sandra.

When Jake first lost his job, Sandra had been supportive—at least, for the most part. It's true that she had accused him of not fighting hard enough for his position, but he had taken that as a sign of her own anxiety about being the sole breadwinner. It's not like Sandra didn't make enough money. She made almost twice as much as Jake. She was driven at work, but that also meant that she sometimes didn't have much energy left for their relationship. As the months passed, Sandra had occasionally made insensitive comments, but nothing major.

Lately, Sandra's behavior had changed. She had begun criticizing Jake for not doing more around the house, for not having dinner ready, and for not keeping things cleaner. She had also begun calling him "lazy." Sandra seemed to resent having to support Jake financially and emotionally. He felt like a huge drag on her.

Last night, Sandra finally snapped. She told Jake that she was tired of "carrying all the weight." She gave him an ultimatum: "Shape up and get your act together or I'm leaving." Jake had been taken completely offguard. Of course he already knew that Sandra felt put-upon by his depression. She never seemed to miss a chance to drive home the point that, at least in her mind, he wasn't doing enough. Nevertheless, he assumed that they could work it out together. After all,

Jake supported Sandra through graduate school. In the months after her mother passed away, Jake was supportive of Sandra during her grief. Now that Jake needed some extra care and support, Sandra only seemed to feel exhausted and inconvenienced. He simply didn't know what to do.

Why Do Narcissists Act This Way?

You can't give what you haven't got. To some extent, you learn to empathize with others by first having others empathize with you. A key concept when it comes to empathy and child development is mirroring. In simple terms, mirroring is when a caregiver notices a child's emotional state and responds appropriately. Children learn to recognize their own emotional states by seeing them reflected on the faces and in the actions of their caregivers. Everyday examples of mirroring include things like returning a baby's smiles, responding to distress with gentle concern and a soothing manner, or mimicking a baby's look of surprise and delight. Mirroring helps people develop self-awareness and make sense of the world. It helps give an individual a sense of being a person whose feelings and experiences have merit and meaning. Basically, mirroring is an essential ingredient in the formation of a stable and positive sense of self.

A teacher once said, "If you raise a child in a closet and shove food under the door, you won't end up with a healthy or functional person." Everyone needs relationships with other people to become fully formed human beings. Relationships (especially in youth) provide context and meaning to thoughts and feelings. They anchor and organize internal experiences. Children who are empathically mirrored grow up feeling secure that they are "seen"— that their thoughts and feelings are comprehensible to others. They feel connected and understood. As Donald Winnicott, a famous psychoanalyst put it, "It is a joy to be hidden, but disaster not to be found." Children who grow up with insufficient mirroring must cope with the continual disaster of never having been found.

So what does it look like when parents do not mirror their children? It's actually quite common and can happen for lots of reasons. Some parents experience relationship turmoil, financial distress, or health issues that preoccupy them and make them less receptive to their child's emotional cues. Unfortunate and sometimes unavoidable events like death or chronic illness can steal the focus from young children, causing them to fade into the background of a stressed or grieving household.

Some parents have mental health issues that make it difficult for them to provide attentive, positive mirroring. People with borderline personality disorder, for instance, have erratic mood swings and, like narcissists, fluctuate between periods of intense idealization and devaluation. This makes it difficult to accurately mirror their child's emotional states. Other issues like severe depression or anxiety can negatively affect the parent-child relationship.

Other Examples of Low Empathy

KICKING OTHERS WHEN THEY'RE DOWN Most people try to tread lightly when someone is going through a tough time. For instance, you probably don't go out of your way to criticize people when they are feeling sad or insecure. You are able to do this because you empathize with others and know that you would not want to be treated insensitively if you were in their shoes. Narcissists, on the other hand, may only be able to provide a perfunctory or fleeting acknowledgment of other people's feelings, followed by a quick return to criticisms or entitled behavior.

DIFFICULTY PROVIDING COMFORT Narcissists aren't very good at providing comfort to others because they have difficulty stepping outside of their own immediate needs, feelings, and concerns. For example, narcissists may happily accept care when they are sick, but then only begrudgingly and half-heartedly return the favor. Similarly, when someone is sad or upset, narcissists may express resentment or exasperation. Of course, none of this stops narcissists from soaking up emotional comfort and support from everyone around them when they are having a hard day.

INCONSIDERATE BEHAVIOR Being considerate of others requires empathy. If a person is unable to understand other people's perspectives, he usually ends up behaving insensitively. As a result of low empathy, narcissists may do things like intrude on people's physical space, make people wait, or make thoughtlessly cruel or insensitive comments.

MAKING OTHERS FEEL INVISIBLE People use empathic mirroring to let their romantic partners know that their feelings are understood. It's also used to connect to family members and friends. In fact, any time you connect with someone, you use mirroring to help bridge the gap between yourself and the other person. For instance, if the other person is sad, you might reflect that sadness in your facial expression and tone of voice. This is how people let others know they are being seen and heard.

Rather than mirroring the child's emotional experience, severely depressed parents may only return a blank or despondent stare. Anxious parents may overreact to even minor upsets. Chronically overreactive, underreactive, or distracted parenting may produce a "distorted mirror" that confuses and distresses developing children, who then internalize an unstable or inconsistent sense of self.

The *Psychodynamic Diagnostic Manual,* a diagnostic handbook for psychotherapists, mentions that many narcissists experience feelings of emptiness or meaninglessness. When mirroring goes awry, children grow into narcissistic adults with a big hole in the center of their being. Seeking the mirroring they never got as children, narcissists are perpetually preoccupied with filling this void. When it comes to empathy, narcissists have little to give because they are too busy trying to get it from others.

Narcissists have low empathy as a result of inadequate mirroring. This also means that they may not be able to provide mirroring to others. Being in a relationship with a narcissist can be a little like being a vampire standing in front of a mirror. There's no reflection. It's like you aren't even there. The narcissist may hear your words and understand their meaning, but the feeling of connection is often lacking, as is the sense that the narcissist is actively considering you and your feelings.

Fueling vs. Defusing: Jake's Story

Dealing with self-serving traits means setting boundaries. Sometimes, people use boundaries to set limits on someone else's behavior, and sometimes people use them to make more space for their own needs and feelings.

Even with adequate social support, depression can be incredibly difficult to overcome. Feelings of hopelessness, worthlessness, and guilt are all symptoms that make it hard to ask for things and to set boundaries. However, if

Jake continues to avoid expressing his feelings and clarifying his needs, it will only cause him to become resentful.

Sandra's behavior suggests a stunning lack of empathy for Jake and his situation. It's possible that Sandra is simply not educated about the reality of depression and is mistaking Jake's symptoms for character flaws like laziness or procrastination. Clinical depression is an illness that cannot simply be "snapped out of." It's not actually up to Jake to "pull himself together." With time, treatment, and support from Sandra, he can recover and start living a full life again, but none of this will happen overnight. Sandra is placing unfair and unreasonable pressure on Jake to do something that he simply can't do. Furthermore, she is doing it at a time when he needs patience and understanding, not ultimatums and blame.

It is up to Jake to set the record straight. Sandra's behavior needs to be confronted, and Jake needs to carve out the space he needs to get well. One way of doing this would be for Jake to arrange for a joint session with Sandra and his therapist. This would allow for them to discuss Jake's needs and Sandra's concerns in a controlled and mediated setting. It would also give Jake's therapist a chance to clear up any misunderstandings that Sandra may have about his condition. Alternatively, Jake could spend some time clarifying his feelings with his therapist, a friend, or by himself (perhaps by writing a list or journal entry). Once he has a better idea of how he is feeling, he can write a letter to Sandra. This letter could be something that he gives her to read, or it could be something that he reads to her. He could ask for her to reserve comment until he has finished.

There is no guarantee that Sandra will change her mind or even be receptive to listening. Setting boundaries isn't about controlling other people's behavior. It's about doing what you can to change what you can. Most importantly, setting boundaries is about being your own advocate and taking care of yourself.

Not only can narcissists be entitled and lack empathy, but sometimes they can be just plain exploitative. The next chapter will look at why and how narcissists exploit others, and what you can do about it.

CHAPTER 7

Is Exploitative of Others

Exploitation means using others to satisfy your own needs and desires. People can exploit others financially by taking advantage of their kindness, generosity, or naïveté, and getting them to buy things that they may not actually be able to afford. People can exploit others' bodies by treating them as sexual objects. People can exploit others emotionally by using their feelings to get them to behave in certain ways. Basically, exploitation happens any time a person takes advantage of someone else.

It's often easy to spot overt exploitation, like when an employer leverages a poor job market to get employees to work long hours with lower pay, or when a large corporation exploits natural resources and harms the environment. If people aren't adequately sensitized, many subtle forms of exploitation escape attention. In everyday relationships, exploitation may involve playing on a person's insecurities to manipulate behavior. Exploitation can even happen unintentionally. For instance, therapists must be trained to be vigilant of their own behavior in psychotherapy to protect their patients against unintended exploitation. Patients come to therapy in a vulnerable state and must rely on the professional ethics and expertise of the therapist. Even well-trained therapists can unwittingly exploit patients whose insecurities make them overly compliant and eager to please. For example, therapists can give themselves permission to be late to sessions, frequently cancel on short notice, or pressure their patients for compliments or positive feedback.

Mary's Story

"Are you sure you want to wear that?" Mary's mother asked as they were getting ready to leave for a Fourth of July barbecue. "It makes you look like a hippie, and red makes you look flushed." Mary looked down at her red sundress. Until about 30 seconds ago, she had felt quite proud of it. Now, a seed of doubt had been planted in her mind.

Mary was used to her mother's critiques. For as long as she could remember, her mother had made comments and suggestions about her appearance. Getting ready for school used to be a nightmare. Mary could remember feeling constantly anxious and unsure. Throughout grade school, her mother would pick her outfits. Finally, when Mary was in the tenth grade, she had mustered enough courage to insist that she pick out her own clothes each morning for school. Her mother begrudgingly complied, but to this day continued to make critical comments.

Through years of therapy, Mary had gradually come to realize that her mother was actually worried about her own image. Her mother felt embarrassed if Mary didn't look good. Understanding this had made a big difference to Mary's self-esteem. Before, she simply took it for granted that not looking perfect was a disaster of epic proportions. Now, she realized that it simply felt like a disaster to her mother. Nevertheless, Mary still felt insecure about herself when she wore a new outfit that hadn't received her mother's stamp of approval. Old habits die hard.

Now that Mary had a family of her own, she had begun to realize just how damaging critical remarks about appearance could be. She didn't want her children growing up feeling insecure about themselves and their bodies. Mary wanted to put an end to her mother's critical comments before her children were old enough to really be affected by them. She had begun to think it was time to set a boundary in their relationship.

Why Do Narcissists Act This Way?

Stephen Johnson, psychologist and author of the book *Humanizing the Narcissistic Style*, calls narcissists "used children." This phrase captures the exploitative nature of the early care relationships thought to cause narcissism. In Johnson's perspective, people become narcissistic when parents or caregivers exploit their children to maintain their own self-esteem at the expense of the child's developmental needs. Narcissists grow to repeat this cycle of exploitation throughout their lives. Johnson's ideas are similar to those of other prominent thinkers on the subject. In *The Drama of the Gifted Child*, Swiss psychologist and psychoanalyst Alice Miller wrote, "What happens if a mother not only is unable to recognize and fulfill her child's needs, but is herself in need of assurance? Quite unconsciously, the mother then tries to assuage her own needs through her child . . . the mother often loves her child passionately, but not in the way he needs to be loved. The reliability, continuity, and constancy that are so important for the child are therefore missing from this exploitative relationship." This theme of parental exploitation of the child for his ability to reflect positively on the parent recurs throughout the literature on narcissism. It is sometimes conceptualized as the original narcissistic injury that causes the child to develop the defenses of grandiosity and vanity, disables the child's empathy, and makes the child vulnerable to periods of depression, anxiety, and shame throughout his or her life.

Imagine, for a moment, how it feels when someone takes advantage of you. Everyone has been there; perhaps it was a boss, friend, teacher, or ex-lover. Try to remember the sense of shock and betrayal when you realized that someone who had pretended to care did not actually have your best interests at heart. This is a glimpse into the abhorrent reality of children who are used narcissistically by their parents. It can take years of treatment to work through the resulting feelings of anger and grief. The process is often complicated by the fact that the exploitation may have happened at the hands of otherwise well-intentioned parents who simply didn't know any better. Well-intentioned or not, narcissistic exploitation is the genesis of the false self—the mask that narcissists wear in an attempt to be the person they believe others want them to be. One narcissistic patient had been raised by a mother who idealized him as the only good thing she had ever done. Having suffered an abusive upbringing herself, this mother used her child to prove to herself that she was worth something. Throughout his childhood, she placed both subtle and overt pressure on him to live up to her expectations and become the person she needed him to be to vindicate herself. Sometimes, this pressure took the form of unrealistic adoration that filled the patient with inflated ideas about his own potential. For instance, she would tell him that he might be the "second coming of Jesus." Instead of realistic, positive, and consistent mirroring, the patient's mother provided a distorted mirror reflecting her own narcissistic need to produce a perfect child. If the patient behaved in a way that contradicted this fantasy, he would be punished severely, either through the use of force or by the sudden withdrawal of all love and affection. As a result, he learned to produce the image his mother needed to see—in effect, he mirrored her. His authentic self went underground, eventually becoming lost even to himself. This patient's self-esteem was damaged and unstable due to his mother's idealizations and harsh reprisals for disappointing her. Part of him was unrealistically inflated, and part of him was ashamed and afraid of abandonment. This patient's upbringing had made him dependent on constant reassurance that he was good and perfect. As an adult, when such feedback was lacking, he would start to feel anxious, aimless, and depressed. These feelings echoed the earlier punishments and emotional abandonment suffered at the hands of his mother. Having been raised in an exploitative relationship in which he was used for someone else's self-esteem needs, this patient unconsciously repeated patterns of exploitation with others. Romantic partners and friends were milked for the adoration and idealization he craved and tossed to the curb if they didn't provide him with an adequate supply of self-esteem. It was only after years of treatment that this patient began to recognize the ways that he was exploiting others. Eventually, he was able to confront the abuse that he had suffered at the hands of his well-meaning but narcissistic mother. This is the sort of work that eventually allows narcissists to recover.

Other Examples of Exploitative Behavior

USING OTHERS Although they may not realize it, narcissists often use others for positive mirroring and emotional support without giving much in return. They may demand that people drop everything to provide undivided attention, or may become angry when others don't provide enough praise. When ability or willingness to provide this support and reassurance runs out, the narcissist may move on to someone else who can provide the emotional resources they seek.

Narcissists also use others as sources of self-esteem. This includes choosing partners they feel will make them look good to others, or attempting to get close to successful people to bask in their limelight.

Some narcissists battle feelings of unimportance and insecurity by helping people who are worse off. While this may seem like a positive and even charitable trait, it is actually a way of using others. This is because narcissists help others in a self-serving way that demands attention, recognition, and gratitude.

PRESSING AN ADVANTAGE Narcissists are hungry for praise, approval, and success. Playing fair is not a top priority. When given an advantage over someone else, it's a pretty safe bet that they will use it to get the ›

❭ CONTINUED

narcissistic supply they crave. It's not so much that narcissists make conscious choices to throw others under the bus; the need to win outweighs all other consider-ations. Examples include cheating in games, "stacking the deck" in competitive situations, or "going for the jugular" in relationship arguments by saying or doing things that feel cruel and heavy-handed.

ABUSING A POWER DIFFERENTIAL This is similar to pressing an advantage, but involves situations where narcissists have legitimate power over others. Managers, police officers, and teachers are examples of this kind of authority position. When narcissists are placed in posi-tions of authority, they may exploit their power by acting out insecurities and forcing others to gratify them.

For instance, a narcissistic police officer can coerce people into showing gratuitous displays of respect, and a manager could punish an employee for expressing opin-ions they don't like. More subtle forms of abuse of power can include parents exerting pressure on their children to think and act like them rather than develop their own personalities and interests.

Fueling vs. Defusing: Mary's Story

Mary has lived with her mother's controlling insecurity for most of her life. She's won a few major battles, such as picking out her own clothes in high school, but she will have to continue setting boundaries to minimize the amount of emotional space taken up by her mother's critical comments.

Currently, there's no room for Mary's unique identity; it's all about her mother's attempts to deal with her own insecurities. However unconsciously done, Mary's mother is actually using Mary to deal with her own issues. The control and criticism have already injured Mary, requiring her to seek therapy. If Mary wants to take care of herself and her children, she will have to set a boundary.

The best time to confront narcissistic individuals is when things are calm. Attempting to have a talk about problematic behavior in the heat of the moment will likely only be met with rage or defensive stonewalling. Narcissists are sensitive to criticism. They absolutely hate having their mistakes pointed out. By waiting until things are calm, you stand a better chance of being heard.

Waiting until things are calm gives you an opportunity to frame the discussion. Narcissists want to be good at things. Mary could say something like, "I'd really like to talk about something, but I'm afraid it might make you angry. Can I ask you to listen to me for a few minutes before responding?" This reverse psychology gives her mother a sense that getting angry and interrupting would be the wrong thing to do. Priding herself on being generous, patient, and understanding (even if she is really none of those things), Mary's mother may try very hard to comply with the request and listen quietly.

Mary could then go on to acknowledge her mother's good taste and concern for her family. If she is careful to give her mother credit for having good intentions, her mother is less likely to feel threatened. She could say something like, "Ever since I was young, I've looked up to you as a person with a good sense of style and good taste. I know how important it is to you that the people you care about look good. You've always tried to look out for me in that way. But sometimes, it can feel like a bit much. Sometimes, without meaning to, you make comments that cause me to feel bad about myself—having the opposite effect of what I think you intend. Now that I'm a mom, I want my kids to feel good about themselves and confident that they can make good choices. I've decided that I want to let them learn from their own mistakes and express their own creative identities. I want to request that you refrain from making comments about how I or the children look. This is really important to me; so important, that I really must insist."

If her mother responds by escalating or criticizing her, Mary should remain calm and neutral. She should restate matter-of-factly that this is what she wants and that her mother can choose whether or not to honor her request. If she chooses not to honor her request, then Mary will have to consider how much time she and her children spend in her mother's company.

When setting boundaries, it's important to remember that you can't control someone else's behavior. Mary's mother is free to respond to Mary's request in any way that she wants. Her decision is entirely up to her. When setting a boundary, your only job is to state clearly what you want (or what you don't want) and then be willing to follow through. Actions speak louder than words. If Mary's mother chooses not to respect her boundary, then Mary must choose whether or not she spends as much time with someone who refuses to honor her wishes and feelings.

CHAPTER 8

Dealing with Self-Serving Behavior

Self-serving behaviors shift the boundaries between you and the narcissist. To use an everyday metaphor, think about property lines. *Entitled* behaviors shift the property line into your backyard, giving the narcissist more room than she really needs, while *low empathy* basically ignores your property altogether. *Exploitative* behaviors are like someone using your property to throw a wild party. If a neighbor treated your property this way, you'd probably erect a fence, put up signs, or even call the police. Dealing with self-serving behaviors means taking steps to protect your emotional property.

Setting Boundaries

Assertiveness can be a scary word to people who don't have much practice setting boundaries. Many people think assertiveness involves being mean, angry, or confrontational.

While it's true that assertive behavior sometimes means having a confrontation, it more often just means you are protecting your rights. In relationships, you have the right to be treated in ways that feel good. Being in a functional relationship means that you respect the rights of others, and they respect your rights in return. Understanding the differences between passive, aggressive, and assertive behavior can help you think about setting healthy boundaries.

Passive behavior is when a person allows someone to abuse their rights. Some examples of passive behavior include not speaking up when someone takes advantage of you, or not saying no when someone asks for something that you can't afford. When you behave passively, you are setting yourself up to become angry, frustrated, and depressed. Although it is often easier in the short-term, passive behavior ends up hurting everyone involved. Have you ever known someone who let their dog or cat run the entire household? Odds are, neither the person nor their pet was very happy. Pets need boundaries. They need to know their place in the household to feel safe and well adjusted. Just as animals that are allowed to run amok are not happy, so are people who are allowed to do whatever they please. Healthy relationships require a balance among the rights of everyone involved.

Aggressive behavior is on the other end of the scale. When people are aggressive, they trample the rights of others for personal gain. This can include verbally abusive behavior, such as talking down to wait staff or retail clerks, or controlling behavior, such as restricting a spouse's finances against her will. When people behave aggressively, they create problems for everyone involved. Although aggressive behavior may get your immediate needs met, it comes at the price of creating animosity and resentment in others. Nobody likes to be bullied. People naturally rebel against feeling controlled or abused. When people habitually behave aggressively, they often end up alone.

Like Goldilocks in the well-known fairy tale, there has to be a middle ground. Put simply, assertiveness is "just right." Assertive behavior protects and honors the rights of everyone involved. When you behave assertively, you choose not to let others abuse you or take away your rights, and you do so in a way that respects the rights of others. The beauty of assertiveness is that it doesn't require you to control anyone else's behavior. You can't make someone like you or respect your wishes. Attempting to do so would be aggressively taking away that person's rights. All you can do is set limits and be willing to follow through when those limits are challenged. Sometimes, following through means setting the limit again. Sometimes, it means getting a person of authority involved, like the police, a boss or manager, or even taking someone to court. Sometimes, it simply means walking away from someone whose behavior has become abusive. Assertiveness never requires you to yell, intimidate, or use physical force. It never requires you to get the upper hand with someone, or do anything that would be harmful to yourself or someone else.

As you may have already suspected, self-serving behaviors usually fall under the aggressive category because they are attempts to diminish your rights. Here are some tips for setting boundaries in different types of relationships where you might encounter them.

Partner or Ex-Partner

Because people often look to romantic partners for comfort, empathy, and safety, self-serving behaviors can be especially painful in intimate relationships. When you find yourself in a relationship with someone who has narcissistic tendencies, empathy and consideration may be in short supply.

One way of approaching the issue of self-serving behaviors in intimate (and ex-intimate) relationships is to do a little bit of front-loading. Front-loading is working to change a problematic behavior (or encourage a positive one) before the behavior occurs. Instead of reacting to the behavior after it has already happened, you work up front to prevent it. Narcissists are worried about being seen, understood, and validated. They are often reluctant to step outside their comfort zone unless it feels safe. If you are looking for consideration from a narcissistic partner, you might consider putting in a little bit of extra effort up front to make sure that this person feels seen and appreciated. This can include small things, like little love notes in the morning, neck rubs in the evening, and small, reassuring comments throughout the day. Little statements like "I appreciate you" or "I know how stressed out you've been lately" can actually go a long way toward getting you the consideration you need in return. If you're dealing with an ex-partner, proactive, positive statements can work to foster goodwill and mutual consideration.

While front-loading is helpful for getting that little bit of extra consideration, it may not be enough if you are dealing with overt entitlement, low empathy, or exploitation. Sometimes, you need to set a boundary. Try thinking about what you need and what's been missing. Make a list if it's helpful. Clarify what's important to you in terms of your relationship. Think about the compromises you'd be willing to make, and what's definitely off-limits. Have a contingency plan. What will you do if the person refuses to acknowledge or respect your boundary? What would constitute a deal-breaker? By doing this work up front, you can be more prepared to set an assertive boundary when problematic behavior occurs.

Parent

When a parent engages in self-serving behaviors, the behaviors have a long history that stretches back into childhood. Typically, setting boundaries is way overdue. Parents are supposed to place their children's needs first. Whether their children are newborns or fully grown, self-serving behavior from parents upsets the natural order. All children, regardless of age, want to be loved and accepted by their parents. When parents use this innate feeling in self-serving ways, it represents an abuse of power that can be truly painful and damaging to self-esteem. As discussed, some theories believe this is actually what causes narcissism in the first place.

Nevertheless, some parents give themselves permission to place their own needs and feelings first. Perhaps they make entitled demands about visits, or monopolize phone conversations by only talking about themselves. Some parents play on their children's feelings of guilt or obligation to coerce them into giving time or money that they can't afford. Rather than facing the difficult prospect of examining their own behavior and making healthy changes, some parents opt to use indirect threats of emotional abandonment to pressure their adult children into harmful and maladaptive relationship patterns.

When dealing with a parent's self-serving behaviors, spend some time thinking about the history behind the behaviors you would like to address. How far back do they go? How have they affected you? How does your parent's self-focus make you feel about yourself? Finally, is this something that you are willing to tolerate for the rest of your relationship?

If the answer to that last question is *no*, then you know that you need to set a boundary. You may feel (understandably) worried or intimidated by the idea of setting a boundary when there may be decades of history behind a particular behavior. Allow your thoughts about that history and what it has cost you to galvanize your resolve to assertively stand up for your rights in the relationship. Remember, you only need to speak your truth and be willing to follow through. You can't change anyone's behavior but your own.

Boss or Coworker

The idea of setting boundaries at work can be intimidating. This is particularly true when the problematic relationship is with a boss or manager. It's unrealistic to think that people in positions of power and authority will never act in entitled or non-empathetic ways. That being said, nobody has to tolerate exploitative or abusive behavior in any setting. It is possible to act assertively at work; just know that in some situations, it may have consequences.

Being assertive means taking responsibility for your own values. If something is important to you, protecting it may cost you something else. For example, refusing to work in the evenings or on weekends may mean losing an upcoming raise or facing a negative performance review. Being clear about what is really important to you takes the guesswork out of setting boundaries in any situation. When you have a clear and well-articulated sense of your own values, protecting them comes naturally. This is true at work and at home. The values clarification exercise at the end of this chapter may help you get a better sense of what is most important in your life. Let those values determine when you are willing to make compromises, and when you need to say "absolutely not."

Healing Techniques

The healing techniques in this chapter are designed to help you clarify values and set boundaries through assertive behavior.

Clarifying Your Values

Just as locking the front door to your house protects the people inside, setting boundaries is all about protecting what is important to you. This exercise will help you identify what you need to protect in your life.

Sit in a comfortable place and close your eyes. Allow yourself to take three to five relaxing breaths. Breathe deeply, letting the air go all the way into your belly, before exhaling gently. When you feel centered, open your eyes and complete the following task.

Make a list of everything that's important to you. It could include family, friends, religious or spiritual beliefs, hobbies, your career, art, and anything else that has personal value and meaning to you. Just let yourself brainstorm. Don't worry about ranking the list and don't worry about whether or not to include some things. If something pops into your mind, put it on the list.

When you feel you've listed enough items, again close your eyes. Now imagine you are on a lifeboat. There's limited space on board this vessel, and only five things will fit. Everything else needs to be thrown overboard. You can only keep the five things that are absolutely necessary for your survival. When you've placed yourself in this scenario,

How to Say "No"

Setting and protecting boundaries means saying "no."
Some find this difficult because they are afraid of being
mean or hurting someone's feelings. Others worry that
their wishes won't be respected. Whatever the reasons,
difficulty saying "no" can lead to big problems in any
relationship.

How do you say "no" in a way that is calm, friendly,
and effective? Here are five simple steps:

1   Clearly state your refusal. There's no need to mince
    words or beat around the bush. If your aim is to say
    "no," then come right out and say it. What's more,
    take responsibility for your refusal. Try saying, "I
    won't do _____," or "I've decided not to do _____,"
    rather than "I can't do _____." Some people take
    the latter as an invitation to convince you that you
    really can do it. If you say "I won't" or "I've decided
    not to," there is much less room for debate. The
    idea is to clearly communicate your intentions.
    You may need to repeat yourself a few times if the
    person isn't accustomed to you setting limits.

2   Under most circumstances, you can stop here. There
    is no need to explain yourself. Saying "no" should

always be enough. However, just refusing someone's request without adding any other explanation can come across as insensitive and abrupt. If you'd like to expand, continue with the following steps.

3 Acknowledge the other person's needs or wishes. People are less likely to argue if they know that you understand the reasons behind their request.

4 Acknowledge the other person's feelings. People like to know that they have been understood and that you can see things from their perspective.

5 State the reason for your refusal. Be as clear as possible.

6 Offer alternatives or compromises.

PUTTING IT ALL TOGETHER A friend asks you for a loan, and you're uncomfortable with lending money. You could say something like, "I've decided not to lend you money. I know that you are in a bind and really need the help. I imagine it was hard coming to a friend to ask for a loan. I'm just not comfortable with the idea, though. If there's some other way I can help, I'd be happy to do so."

If someone argues with your boundary, you only need to restate your refusal in a calm and direct manner. If they persist, tell them that the conversation is over and walk away.

open your eyes and look at your list. You can only keep five items on this list. The rest need to be thrown overboard. It's not that the items thrown overboard aren't important; they just aren't as important as the five items you can keep.

Now look over your five items. These are your core values, the values that you can't do without. These are the areas you need to focus on when setting boundaries. The values thrown overboard are still important, but they represent areas where you may be willing to compromise.

Think about these five core values (if you couldn't come up with five, that's okay—just think about however many you have). Why are these values so important to you? What makes them indispensable? How important is it to protect them? Perhaps your children are on the list, or your marriage. Perhaps you listed self-care, or doing good things for others. Whatever is on that list represents the values that give your life meaning and direction. Are these areas in which you're willing to compromise? Is someone else's behavior threatening these values? Would you be willing to face discomfort, the threat of rejection, or even losing the relationship if it meant protecting one or more of these values?

Getting Cozy with Discomfort

Much of life is spent trying to avoid or control uncomfortable experiences. The brain is really good at identifying sources of discomfort and figuring out how to make things better. People build houses to escape the elements, develop agriculture to avoid hunger, and make clothing to beat the cold. The brain is so good at this that people sometimes get stuck in patterns of avoidance and control—patterns than can cause problems. Maybe you avoid trying new things because you might not like the results, or avoid going places that make you anxious. When the avoiding and controlling parts of the brain are allowed to steer the ship, people settle into unhealthy behavior patterns simply because they are familiar and comfortable.

Setting boundaries, especially ones that challenge years of established relationship patterns, can be very uncomfortable. Discomfort, for many, can be a reason to put off taking action that might result in greater health and happiness down the road. Sometimes you have to say "yes" to discomfort, fear, and anxiety to get unstuck.

Try this: Get an ice cube from the freezer. Hold it in your bare hand. Close your eyes and focus on the sensations. It's helpful to breathe into the feeling of coldness, allowing yourself to really *be* with the discomfort as it slowly turns to pain. Try to recognize that, as uncomfortable or even painful as this sensation may be, it is just a feeling. Although your brain begins to scream that you need to drop the ice cube, practice challenging your brain's advice, even if only for a few moments. Let yourself be right there with the pain. Let yourself get close to it and really feel it. This sensation is harmless, even though the feelings tell you the opposite. Recognize that you are in control of your actions. You can choose to be with discomfort, and you can choose when to let go.

When the pain becomes too much, drop the ice cube. If you can tolerate pain and discomfort for the sake of an exercise in a book, imagine what you can tolerate to protect things that are really important to you. Try to hold this lesson in mind when thinking about setting boundaries. Standing up for your rights will be uncomfortable. It might even be painful. You can choose to be with those unwanted feelings rather than avoid them. It's up to you.

3

PART

The Vanity Dimension

Vanity and narcissism go hand-in-hand. It's difficult to imagine a narcissistic person who isn't in some way concerned about appearances. But vanity isn't just about looking good. Narcissists can be vain about talents, skills, income, or anything else that can confer special status. As with the other aspects of narcissism, vanity is a way to defend against underlying fears and insecurities. For both grandiose and vulnerable narcissists, vanity stems from the need to maintain the false self and keep it from falling apart.

Grandiose narcissists are like people who keep a meticulously clean and well-decorated home, except for one room that is completely full of junk. The junk room is where the order breaks down and chaos reigns. Many grandiose narcissists maintain a beautiful façade. While they may have sculpted bodies, precisely combed hair, or perfect teeth, their outer beauty is not supported by an inner sense of well-being. For those grandiose narcissists who are less concerned with physical beauty, there may be equally well-maintained aspects of their lives. However, there are also those who, even in the absence of superlative traits like beauty, talent, or wealth, simply adopt an attitude of superiority. Whether or not the vanity is justified from an outside perspective, grandiose narcissists all tend to use it in the same way.

For grandiose narcissists, vanity is a way to protect themselves against being overwhelmed by unconscious distress. For some, this inner chaos takes the form of impotent rage that threatens to undermine efficacy and well-being. For others, it consists of dependent longings so fused with shame that they threaten to make it impossible to see anyone or anything as good. Some narcissists have inner distress that is not yet differentiated into identifiable feelings and can only be described as *emptiness*.

Powerless over these inner feelings, grandiose narcissists try to compensate through perfection. They attempt to fuse with their *ideal self*—that is, a perfect vision of themselves. This is actually true for all narcissists, not just the grandiose ones. The main difference lies in the ability of grandiose narcissists to feel like they can achieve the perfection that they seek. Sometimes they feel they've already achieved it and only need to maintain their perfect status.

As discussed, vulnerable narcissists struggle with a false self that feels like it is falling apart. They feel farther and farther out of reach of their ideal self, while sensing that they are in danger of tumbling into the emptiness inside. This struggle typically shows up in the form of symptoms like depression and anxiety. They use vanity to seek reassurance, as opposed to their grandiose counterparts, who tend to use vanity in a more boastful and self-assured manner. For example, instead of admiring themselves in the mirror, vulnerable narcissists are more likely to focus on imperfections. Like the Beast, they feel that their flaws make them unwanted by society.

Vulnerable narcissists are more in touch with the shame and anger that live inside them. However, they are no better at dealing with these feelings than grandiose narcissists are. Instead, they tend to feel powerless and overcome by their feelings. They turn to others for reassurance that they aren't as flawed and worthless as they fear, often placing excessive demands for narcissistic supply on the people they care about.

Neither grandiose nor vulnerable narcissists are able to feel that they have worth outside of what they can do, how much they are liked, or how aligned they feel with an ideal vision of themselves. The next few chapters will take a closer look at such vanity.

CHAPTER 9

Preoccupation with Fantasies

When people talk about preoccupation with fantasies of unlimited success, power, brilliance, beauty, or ideal love, they are really talking about fantasies of perfection. Whether or not the fantasies are talked about, narcissists often harbor unrealistic ideas about just how amazing things could or should be.

For many narcissists, every aspect of life is measured on a scale between worthlessness and perfection. It's common for narcissists to become dissatisfied with relationships because they don't live up to the image of the perfect union they've imagined. Many narcissists also have unrealistic ideas about their bodies. Grandiose narcissists may think they are more attractive than they actually are, while vulnerable narcissists may focus on one or two imperfections that they've blown out of proportion. Most narcissists also have unrealistic ideas about success.

Grandiose narcissists blame others for failure to achieve their potential, while vulnerable narcissists blame themselves. Finally, narcissists may imagine scenarios in which they stridently and confidently overcome all adversity: the coworker they don't like, the boss that denied their raise, the teacher who made them feel foolish, or the romantic interest who declined a date.

This dichotomy between worthlessness and perfection is sometimes called *splitting*. Splitting happens when a person psychologically separates parts of himself, or parts of the world in general, into all-good and all-bad categories. It's thought that people with personality disorders rely on this way of thinking because they have difficulty integrating good and bad categories to gain a more holistic picture of themselves and the world. This inability to hold the good and bad together at the same time results in swings between highs (when everything seems perfect) and lows (when everything seems terrible).

Crystal's Story

Crystal's boyfriend, Jason, ran hot and cold. At times, he seemed larger than life. He was confident, assertive, and funny as hell. He could also be sullen, critical, and insecure. Crystal had even considered the possibility that Jason was bipolar.

When Jason was in a good place, things felt amazing. His exuberance was infectious and made

Crystal feel like she was the perfect girlfriend. He showered her with praise and looked at her with stars in his eyes. Best of all, he wanted to be close. However, Jason could also be a bit of a bully when he was feeling good. He became inflexible about things, and pressured Crystal into acting exactly how he wanted.

Jason's lows were equally infectious. They seemed to follow disappointments. For example, when Jason was passed over for a promotion at work, he became depressed, anxious, and critical. Jason's low periods were difficult for Crystal to endure because Jason would often lash out at her. The way he saw her seemed to change completely. Instead of sexy, beautiful, and cherished, she felt gross, ugly, and picked apart. In times like these, she would dread being around Jason and his seemingly endless well of complaints. Yet, Jason could also be incredibly needy when he felt like this. He would complain that she seemed withdrawn or angry, even if she wasn't. He would accuse her of not loving him anymore. Sometimes he would pick fights for no apparent reason at all.

Crystal didn't know what to think about these two sides of Jason. How could things switch back and forth so drastically? It made her feel crazy. She tried to comfort Jason when he was feeling down, but it was to no avail. He would convince himself that nothing was good enough—not his job, his looks, or even their relationship. Yet when Jason was feeling good, it was *like everything was ideal. He would gush about being on track for a brilliant career and fawn over himself in front of the mirror. Best of all, he would talk about how amazing Crystal looked and how proud he was that they were together. The contrast was truly disorienting.*

Why Do Narcissists Act This Way?

Narcissists are dependent on others for self-esteem. They need constant compliments, reassurances, praise, and admiration. This dependency is immensely threatening to the false self, the mask worn by narcissists to hide their fragile and damaged authentic self. Narcissists fantasize about perfection because being perfect means that you never have to worry about needing anything from anyone ever again. To a narcissist, being perfect means being self-sufficient and therefore safe from shame, anxiety, or fear.

One very specific period of psychological development is thought to predispose people to issues like narcissism. A psychiatrist named Margaret Mahler pioneered work focusing on the period of development when children are first individuating (separating psychologically) from their caregivers. This period is thought to occur during the first two years of life.

Infants are born without any awareness of the separation between themselves and their caregivers. They aren't old enough to realize that mom and dad exist as separate people. As children develop the ability to crawl and then walk, they begin to explore, venturing ever farther from their caregivers. At first, children aren't worried about this separation. They may not even realize that it's there.

After a few months of skinned knees and elbows, children begin to get a sense of their own fragility. They start to realize that the world is a big and dangerous place. Moreover, they begin to notice that physical distance from caregivers also produces a kind of psychological distance, causing anxiety. They try to manage this anxiety by keeping mom or dad in eyesight while exploring. They become tentative, clingy, and constantly check in with trusted caregivers to assure safety and connectedness.

Technically, this stage of development is called the rapprochement subphase of separation-individuation (pronounced *rah-prōsh-mon*, from the French *rapprocher*, meaning "to bring together"). During rapprochement, children seek reassurance from caregivers. It is a delicate period because children must be simultaneously reassured of safety and encouraged to continue individuating. Some parents react by withdrawing reassurance, thinking that tough love will discourage weakness and insecurity. Paradoxically, this often has the opposite effect. Children cannot separate psychologically without adequate reassurance that doing so is safe.

Other caregivers take the opposite approach. Threatened by their child's growing independence, they become stifling and controlling to discourage continued individuation. Either response can disrupt this very important developmental process.

According to some theories, problems that occur during this phase of development contribute to narcissism. When caregivers block or discourage individuation, they force the child to abandon attempts at forming a separate sense of self. He instead invests in a false self that more closely resembles what his caregivers want him to be. Basically, the child's true self can't emerge because to do so requires individuation. Instead, a false self develops that is psychologically tied to caregivers and is dependent on their positive feedback and approval. In some ways, the false self is a psychological extension of the parent. To quote Stephen Johnson in 1987's *Humanizing the Narcissistic Style*, "The child, vulnerable and dependent, will then deny his real self in order to hold onto the mother. Living up to her idealized expectations and ministering to her narcissistic needs, he denies and loses himself. He invests in the idealized false self, trying through it to regain what he lost—the love, respect, echoing, and mirroring which were required for him to discover, accept, and love his true self."

Narcissists can't supply their own validation because they were never able to individuate and decide for themselves what is "good." They need constant feedback that they are succeeding at being the false self. This dependency on others for basic self-esteem is very precarious. The ground may collapse at any time.

Because they could not complete the separation-individuation process, narcissists are forever in search of validation that they are "okay." They want to continue developing, but are stuck with a deep fear of abandonment. Narcissists fantasize about being perfect because the false self is based on being good enough to win parental approval. If they were to achieve perfection, they'd never again have to worry about lacking the approval they need to keep the false self intact.

Fueling vs. Defusing: Crystal's Story

Crystal is struggling with Jason's use of splitting. It's important to remember that splitting is not something that anyone does consciously. It is an unconscious defense mechanism that Jason is unaware of. As a result, he is susceptible to feeling as if things are either good or bad, with little gray area in between. This applies to his view of himself and his view of Crystal. When people are splitting, they often forget that they ever felt any other way. When Jason feels good about himself, he sees everything through a polarizing lens: his job, Crystal, his future, and himself. He forgets ever having felt badly about things because he is literally incapable of connecting to those bad feelings. If reminded of a bad memory, it will suddenly not seem so bad. When Jason is on the "good" side of the split, he idealizes Crystal, who in his eyes becomes a beautiful, sexy woman who can do no wrong. Feelings of limitless potential make Jason feel powerful. Because he suddenly feels capable of getting exactly what he wants out of life, he can become overconfident, arrogant, and even a bit controlling.

Other Examples of Fantasies of Perfection

FANTASIES OF BEING FAMOUS Most people are content with getting a little bit of attention here and there throughout their lives. They don't need to be on the cover of newspapers and magazines to feel that they are worth something. In contrast, many narcissists harbor fantasies that they only need to be "discovered" to enjoy worldwide fame. The fantasy of being imminently visible to everyone is actually a way of compensating for feeling invisible.

FLUCTUATING BETWEEN HIGH AND LOW SELF-ESTEEM As the saying goes, there are two sides to every story. Narcissists often have fantasies that they are (or should be) perfect. This extreme and polarized idea of perfection is highly unrealistic. It warps perception, sending narcissists soaring to the heights of ecstasy when things are going well. If they don't feel perfect, narcissists feel deeply flawed and worthless. Grandiose narcissists often project this feeling onto others in an attempt to rid themselves of it.

FLUCTUATING BETWEEN IDEALIZING AND DEVALUING Narcissists tend to view themselves and the world as either black or white. Imagine you are sorting clothing into boxes. You have a huge pile of clothes—jeans, sweaters, ›

❯ CONTINUED

dresses, socks, underwear, belts—and only two boxes. How do you decide what goes into each box? If you had more boxes, then you could sort based on criteria like color, style, and function. Only having two boxes forces you to see things in a polarized way. Either things go into Box A or into Box B; there's no in-between. Now imagine that Box A is good, and Box B is bad. Every experience— every thought, feeling, and perception—must go into the good box or the bad box. Narcissists fluctuate between feeling perfect and feeling worthless. They both idealize and devalue others. When a narcissist idealizes you, it's as if you've been placed in the good box. Everything about you is, therefore, good. You can do no wrong. It feels amazing to be idealized in this way.

Unfortunately, idealizations never last. They turn into devaluations, because that is the other side of the story. The narcissist will eventually see you are a real person, with morning breath, occasional bad hair days, and a few extra pounds here and there. These "flaws" will eventually force the narcissist to take you out of the good box and put you in the bad box.

However, when Jason is on the "bad" side of the split, everything is thrown in the garbage. He feels worthless, frustrated, and angry. His job is a dead end, Crystal is a flawed and annoying partner, and the world is a cold and unforgiving place. When he's in this state, Jason feels incapable of getting anywhere in life. He feels insecure, and becomes clingy and needy in his relationship with Crystal. Because a part of him is convinced that she is equally full of badness, he questions her intentions and picks fights to prove that she doesn't like him anymore.

Crystal's feelings of disorientation make sense. Splitting can be truly perplexing. It's hard to develop trust when you go from feeling loved and cherished to feeling hated and ugly. Crystal is doomed to fail at improving Jason's mood. No matter how hard she tries, her attempts are filtered through his lens of "badness."

People with personality disorders tend to rely heavily on reality-distorting defenses like splitting and projection. In relationships, splitting tends to cause the most damage when the non-splitting partner takes things personally. If Crystal joins Jason in erasing the other side of the story, she'll be taken for a wild ride between his highs and lows. Instead, she needs to try to occupy the middle ground that Jason has trouble finding. One way to think about this is to imagine a toddler in the middle of a tantrum. Toddlers are notorious splitters. In fact, splitting is a primary coping technique during the first several years of life. Most people develop more mature coping techniques as they grow and develop, but everyone still uses splitting from time to time—particularly when emotions run high. When toddlers tantrum, they may scream that they hate you or that they never want to see you again. As an adult, you can simultaneously hold the other side of the story—that the toddler needs and loves you. If Crystal can take a similar stance in response to Jason's splitting, she can resist being drawn into Jason's distorted experience.

In addition to a preoccupation with fantasies of unlimited success, power, brilliance, beauty, or ideal love, narcissists also require much in the way of praise and attention. The next chapter looks at a second trait of narcissism's vanity dimension: the need for excessive admiration.

CHAPTER 10

Requires Excessive Admiration

Most narcissists need admiration. While they don't necessarily need people to fawn over them, they do require unambiguous positive attention to counteract deeply held insecurities. They are often attracted to jobs and positions that give them authority and influence over others. These sorts of jobs supply high levels of compliments, praise, and attention. For this reason, you are likely to find a greater number of narcissists who are actors, performers, teachers, members of the clergy, authors, therapists, or politicians. You may also recognize some narcissists in your various newsfeeds on social media sites.

Tanya's Story

Tanya was growing tired of Jessica's posts online. At first, she had humored Jessica because they were old friends. When Jessica would post pictures of herself in new clothes, with a new haircut, or with her nails painted a different color, Tanya had joined others in making positive comments. She figured that maybe Jessica was going through a difficult time and needed a self-esteem boost. But as weeks turned into months, Jessica's constant pulls for attention showed no signs of slowing. Lately, in addition to selfies, Jessica had added grandstanding political comments and excessive, self-congratulatory posts to her repertoire. Just last night, Jessica gave herself kudos for compromising with her partner about what to watch on television.

In any other situation, Tanya would have simply ignored this annoying behavior. She certainly had other friends who posted things that bothered her. But Jessica's online antics were different. She had become a bully. When Tanya didn't comment, Jessica would send passive-aggressive online messages or make belligerent comments on Tanya's posts. Tanya found herself feeling pressured to praise Jessica whenever she posted anything, regardless of how ridiculous it was.

Tanya was hesitant to block Jessica online. She didn't want things to be awkward. They grew up together and still lived in the same town. Jessica had always been a bit needy and insecure, but her online activity had taken these traits to new extremes. She was like a bottomless pit of need, always asking for reassurance, compliments, and attention. Tanya was starting to resent feeling so pressured to play along.

Tanya wanted to say something before things got out of control. She didn't want to end up hating Jessica, but she couldn't think of any way to set boundaries without coming across like a bad friend. She didn't want to be insensitive, but Jessica was really getting on her nerves. She was afraid that one of these days, she would snap and say something she would later regret.

Why Do Narcissists Act This Way?

Perhaps the best way to understand a narcissist's need for admiration is to take a look at a related issue: the need for reassurance. Narcissists are constantly struggling to be good enough. Remember the rapprochement phase of development discussed in the last chapter? As you may recall, it involves the child's need for reassurance while individuating (becoming a psychologically separate being). As the theory goes, narcissists never made it through this phase, remaining psychologically tied to others.

When narcissists go too long without some form of reassurance, they begin to feel those old pangs of abandonment anxiety, as if they were back in that early rapprochement scenario. Experiencing the terrifying feeling of psychological distance again, they try to find the reassurance they need to feel reconnected. They long to receive praise so that they can again feel "good." As long as they are good, they don't need to worry about abandonment. Remember, all of this is unconscious and taking place without the narcissist's awareness.

How Can Anyone Know About the Unconscious?

You may wonder how anyone could know what goes on inside someone else's unconscious mind. After all, there aren't any reliable ways to measure or test for unconscious conflicts. This is the sort of problem that researchers run into when they try to understand personality structure, or how people are put together. Often, the best information about personality comes from reports by psychologists who specialize in working with particular issues with many patients over long periods of time.

When psychologists spend years talking to individuals about their lives, thoughts, fantasies, and feelings, they begin to get a sense of how people operate. They notice patterns in behavior and even in the therapy relationship itself. They recognize familiar defense mechanisms, and listen just as closely to what patients *aren't* saying as they do to what they *are* saying. All of this information allows psychologists to make inferences about what is going on under the surface. They form hypotheses, and then test these hypotheses by making interpretations and seeing how people react.

There are nearly 100 years of clinical case material on narcissism to shed light on this very complex issue.

Across the many books published on the subject, there is a consensus that narcissism stems from early experiences and that narcissists have characteristic psychological and emotional conflicts. For psychologists, narcissism isn't just a label. It's a term that means something very specific about a person's personality structure and the types of issues that show up repeatedly in that person's life.

Sometimes, their anxieties about inadequacy show up in surprising ways. For instance, many narcissists have excessive worries about their health. The technical term for this kind of anxiety is illness anxiety disorder (called hypochondriasis prior to the DSM-5). Narcissists may fret about having cancer, AIDS, or other devastating health conditions. Often, these anxieties feel unbearable, necessitating frequent visits to the doctor or demands for unnecessary medical tests.

Narcissists secretly feel that they are not good enough— indeed, that they are deeply flawed. Inside, they feel messy, ashamed, vulnerable, insecure, angry, and sad. Although most narcissists are not consciously aware of these feelings, they may have a vague sense that something is wrong. When people have upsetting feelings that they can't pin down, it often causes anxiety. With illness anxiety disorder, the mind attempts to make sense of the anxiety by attaching it to the possibility of physical illness. The narcissist thinks, "Maybe I feel like something is wrong because my body is breaking down. Maybe I'm sick and I just don't know it yet."

Once you understand why narcissists need reassurance, it is an easy jump to understand the need for excessive admiration. Admiration is really just a form of reassurance. Admiration tells you that you did a good job. It tells you that you are liked or even envied, leaving little room for doubt. That positive attention can be used to get a respite from your own anxieties and insecurities.

Depending on the severity of a person's narcissism, the need for admiration may appear as a slight pull for regular reassurances, or a bullying demand for full-blown praise and worship. The difference largely depends on the person's level of grandiosity.

Fueling vs. Defusing: Tanya's Story

Jessica is pressuring Tanya and other online friends to give her a steady flow of narcissistic supply. People who have developed healthy ways of getting their needs met tend to ask for things directly. They are able to weather disappointment and frustration with grace and maturity. In contrast, people with personality issues tend to ask for things in indirect or ambiguous ways (although this isn't always the case; they can also make very direct demands). They may lash out if their needs aren't met, causing those around them to feel pressured into doing what they want the next time around.

Although Tanya and Jessica are old friends, Tanya is now experiencing understandable frustration and resentment in the face of Jessica's narcissism. It's not fun when someone's insecurities take up too much space in a relationship. Healthy adult relationships require balance and mutual consideration. Tanya is definitely not getting either from Jessica's online behavior.

Traits in the vanity dimension are often about extremes. Jessica's online behavior is about counteracting the fear of being invisible. She fishes for compliments because she is afraid of being worthless. When people don't give her what she wants, they become worthless to her and she lashes out at them.

Narcissists want to be the prettiest, smartest, and most talented. They tend to practice splitting—seeing others as good or bad, with no in-between. When dealing with these traits, it helps to stay anchored in the middle. Nevertheless, it can be difficult to avoid being sucked into the narcissist's distorted worldview. Tanya can't get anywhere with Jessica if she is pulled into Jessica's polarized mentality. For instance, she could start to hate Jessica and talk behind her back. However, joining Jessica in her splitting will only make Tanya feel angry and helpless in the long run. Instead, she needs to set an assertive boundary and refrain from seeing Jessica as all good or all bad.

Other Examples of Excessive Need for Admiration

FISHING FOR COMPLIMENTS Narcissists fish for compliments to replenish their narcissistic supply. Narcissists have great difficulty generating their own good feelings about themselves, forcing them to turn to others for compliments and positive feedback. Everyone does this from time to time. It is perfectly normal for people to seek praise and compliments when they are feeling down about themselves. Narcissists, on the other hand, may engage in this behavior excessively, causing others to feel pressured and even coerced into giving them compliments to avoid negative repercussions.

EXHIBITIONISTIC BEHAVIOR Although commonly associated with public or highly visible sexual behavior, here exhibitionism means any behavior done for attention. Anyone who's spent time around toddlers knows just how exhibitionistic they can be. Toddlers are just discovering themselves, and delight in sharing these discoveries with parents, family, and even strangers they meet at the store. When toddlers strut around the house with a rag on their head, or tear off all of their clothes and laugh hysterically while running naked through the house, they are seeking admiration. They want others to notice them and share in their delight. Over time, these experiences become important sources of narcissistic supply and self-esteem.

When narcissists behave in an exhibitionistic manner, they are seeking the same sort of admiration as toddlers, and for the same reasons. They want attention. This behavior comes in many forms, but all of them have the common feature of demanding attention from others. Some examples include inappropriate dress, talking too loudly, or gesturing in expansive and space-intruding ways.

BOASTING OR SHOWING OFF This trait is a close relative of exhibitionism. Narcissists are notorious for boasting, bragging, and showing off. In part, they do this because they can't feel content that they've done something well without seeking confirmation from as many people as possible. In addition, narcissists sometimes boast because they are trying to represent themselves in the best possible light.

To start, she might consider reducing her active participation in Jessica's online behaviors by commenting less or refraining from commenting altogether. When Jessica notices Tanya's withdrawal (which she surely will), Tanya can try playing it off casually by saying something like, "I saw your post but didn't get around to commenting." She should be careful not to apologize for not commenting because it isn't something for which she is actually sorry.

She should also be careful not to provide a compliment after the fact. If Jessica directly asks for a compliment, she can say something positive but short, like "it looks great." The point is to continue reducing her amount of participation until she is rarely commenting. If Jessica confronts her, Tanya can be honest but neutral. She might say something like, "I enjoy our friendship and think highly of you, but sometimes I feel pressured to give compliments when you make posts. I don't like how that feels." If Tanya can hold the middle ground, she may be able to set a new norm in the relationship.

Beyond a preoccupation with fame and a need for admiration, one final trait underscores the vanity dimension of narcissism: envy.

CHAPTER 11

Feelings of Envy

Because they are always comparing themselves to others, narcissists often struggle with feelings of envy. This envy stems from inner feelings of impoverishment, causing them to covet what others have (e.g., a high income, a seemingly perfect relationship, popularity).

Narcissists may also project these feelings and believe that others are envious of them. The idea that people are secretly envious helps narcissists feel more secure about themselves. After all, envy and admiration are close relatives. People envy those who have things they want. In addition, the idea that people are envious transforms rejection into an underhanded compliment. Instead of thinking "nobody likes me," narcissists can think "people are just envious of me."

Donica's Story

Donica's husband, Marcel, seemed to have an unhealthy fixation on a rival real estate agent named

Tom. By every measure, Marcel was a success. He was competitive in his market, earned a decent income for their family, and seemed to be well liked and respected among his peers. Nevertheless, Marcel talked constantly about Tom.

Marcel called Tom his archnemesis. Marcel had never really liked him. He felt that Tom was uppity and condescending. The two met in college, where they shared a few classes. Marcel had always felt that Tom was one step ahead of him. He'd always gotten slightly better grades, made better arguments in class, and seemed to be better liked than Marcel.

A few years ago, Donica and Marcel had been enjoying lunch at a local restaurant when Marcel suddenly dropped his fork and pointed to the park across the street. "I can't believe it," he whispered. "It's Tom." Over the next year, the two of them experienced more Tom sightings, until it became undeniable that Tom had relocated to their town. Shortly thereafter, Marcel came home with a flyer clenched in his fist. It was Tom's advertisement for a local home sale. "He's a real estate agent, and my competitor!" Marcel raged.

Since then, Marcel was constantly comparing himself to Tom, who still always seemed to be one step ahead. Donica sometimes thought Marcel's rivalry was silly, but other times she felt it bordered on obsessive. Marcel would rant about how Tom was stealing clients from him, about how he had weaseled his way into

*the local professional organization, and about how
much everyone seemed to like Tom. He would fume,
"Am I the only one in the world who knows what a
jerk he is?"*

*Donica was also struck by their similarities. Marcel
and Tom were about the same height, each with a
slender build. Both had dark hair and handsome features. They had even grown up in the same general
area, although they hadn't met until college. It seemed
like they were spun from the same cloth. She wondered
how Tom felt about Marcel.*

*All of this might be funny if it weren't for the effect
it was having on Marcel and their marriage. Lately, it
seemed that Marcel couldn't do anything without first
comparing himself to Tom. He talked about it constantly, to the point that Donica began to dread their
conversations. Whenever Donica would attempt to be
the voice of reason, Marcel would accuse her of not
supporting him. She felt stuck. She wanted for Marcel
to move on and forget about Tom, but she didn't
know how to talk to him about it without it turning
into a disaster.*

Why Do Narcissists Act This Way?

People talk about being "green with envy" because envy is
considered an ugly, shallow emotion. Despite envy's bad
reputation, some of the most painful stories narcissists
tell are about envy—not so much feeling envy because

someone has a nice car or a full head of hair, but envy because others get to be real people while the narcissist feels like a hollow fraud.

Human beings are hardwired to be social. Forming strong social bonds is part of the reason humans came to dominate this planet. Most people don't do well in extended isolation. Humans need to feel affiliated, accepted, and seen. Yet many narcissists feel completely alone. They yearn for acceptance. But like wannabes at an exclusive event, they end up standing around outside, craning their necks to catch a glimpse of the party.

One person described feeling like there was always a part of her that was watching, monitoring her thoughts and behavior to make sure that she wasn't in danger of feeling shame or embarrassment. While everyone else was able to participate fully in life, she was always one step removed. Another person talked about feeling like everyone around him had real relationships while he always felt like a tagalong. He didn't feel like he really *belonged*. A third person talked about constantly feeling ugly and unwanted, envious of those who seemed to feel comfortable around others.

While narcissists' envy may appear to be about money, looks, charm, or popularity on the surface, a deeper look reveals that narcissists are envious of others because they don't have to wear a mask. They want to know what it is like to have a real self. They envy those who can find acceptance for who they really are. Unfortunately, most narcissists have been wearing masks for so long that the real face underneath is undefined. They have a sense that taking off the mask would represent an enormous loss of identity. They fear it would cause a breakdown that they couldn't survive. Imagine having to tear your house down to fix a problem with the plumbing. It seems like such a huge task—so large that you might just try to get by with bad plumbing. Most narcissists have an unconscious fantasy that fixing what is wrong would require them to lose themselves completely. In fact, the opposite is usually the case. Treating narcissism is all about finding the true self and encouraging it to grow.

Fueling vs. Defusing: Donica's Story

When dealing with problematic narcissistic behavior, it's easy to tiptoe around issues to avoid conflict. In each of the stories in Part 3, the recommended course of action has been to confront the problematic behavior while still maintaining solid footing in the middle. Marcel is idealizing Tom's life while simultaneously turning him into a villain—going so far as to claim he is Marcel's archnemesis. In all likelihood, Tom has no idea that Marcel has created this dramatic narrative about their relationship. Tom probably doesn't even know that Marcel is envious of him. Marcel's preoccupation with Tom shouldn't be a big deal, except that it has begun to create problems in his relationship with Donica.

Other Examples of Issues with Envy

A SENSE THAT LIFE IS UNFAIR When dealing with disappointments, many narcissists have an external locus of control, meaning that they feel controlled by external influences. This perspective protects narcissists from having to look at their own faults and failings. For example, if a narcissist doesn't get a job promotion, she might explain it as "bad luck" instead of thinking about how to do better next time. While this perspective protects narcissists from feeling at fault when bad things happen, it also leaves them feeling as if life is unfair.

FEELINGS OF BITTERNESS Bitterness is an emotional response to feeling wronged. Most people take disappointment in stride. Maybe you've learned not to take it personally when things don't work out the way you'd hoped. Even if you are envious of someone, you most likely don't feel bitter toward that person because you recognize that the world won't simply hand you everything you want.

In contrast, narcissists feel entitled to the things they want, leaving them bitter toward others when things don't work out. For example, narcissists may feel entitled to popularity and therefore despise others who are well liked. In the performing arts, a common stereotype involves the bitter and envious understudy who hates the lead actor or actress of the show.

OBSESSION OR PREOCCUPATION WITH CERTAIN PEOPLE Narcissists may have one or two people that they consider to be "just like them." This phenomenon is called twinship transference and stems from the narcissist's use of others for positive mirroring. By finding themselves in another person, they can use that identification to help regulate their own self-concept. For instance, it is not uncommon to hear narcissistic individuals refer to others as soulmates. They imagine that the other person thinks and feels just like they do, often forming strong feelings of attachment and affection. However, these feelings aren't always positive. Narcissists can also envy their "twin," seeing that person as an imposter who somehow stole the life to which the narcissist feels entitled.

When Donica attempted to discuss these issues with Marcel in the past, he became angry. Marcel is already hypersensitive to feeling inadequate when compared to Tom. It might even be fair to say that Marcel becomes a bit paranoid, thinking that Tom is somehow attempting to undermine his success. This insecurity and paranoia extend to Donica when Marcel perceives her as standing against him. Marcel's reactivity to these issues discouraged

Donica from setting boundaries that would feel better to her in the relationship. If Donica wants things to change, she'll have to speak up about her feelings.

People with problematic personality traits are often allowed to get away with outrageous treatment of others because they react so strongly when confronted. However, problematic behavior never changes if it isn't confronted. It can be tricky to see the distortions behind severe emotional responses that involve splitting. In Donica's case, she may actually feel guilty of not supporting Marcel. She may worry that Marcel will retaliate if she attempts to hold him accountable for his behavior. Donica needs to be able to hold a balanced, rational, adult perspective when it comes to this issue. She should approach Marcel in a calm, neutral way and express her feelings, rather than criticize his behavior. If he attempts to criticize or blame her, she might try saying something like, "You may not be able to see how I'm on your side, but I am. I want to be close to you, and your feelings about Tom are getting in the way. It seems to you like I am withdrawing from you, but you are actually withdrawing from me by devoting so much time and energy to Tom." Donica might also consider suggesting that Marcel seek counseling. It could help him sort through his feelings about Tom and give him space to discuss them as openly as he wants. If Donica can consistently confront Marcel in this manner without losing herself to his splitting, she may be able to set a new precedent in their relationship.

CHAPTER 12

Dealing with Vanity

If you can understand the practice of splitting, then you are well on your way to being more effective at dealing with the majority of problematic human behavior. Traits in the vanity dimension involve the narcissist placing pressure on you to join him in splitting the world into idealized (perfect or "good") and devalued (worthless or "bad") categories. These labels reflect internal divisions that live within the narcissist. Everything that is not ideal is worthless. Narcissists seek assurance that you see them as perfect. They want you to admire or envy them. This constant pressure takes up a lot of emotional space in any relationship. It can also have the effect of destabilizing how you see yourself and the world. Just like spending too much time around someone who complains all the time can make you feel frustrated, pessimistic, and powerless, being in a relationship with someone who relies on splitting can cause you to begin to see yourself and others in shades of black and white.

Be Aware of the Poles

Polarized thinking and feeling can have unexpected effects. You may find yourself feeling less confident, more paranoid, and even more afraid than usual. Sometimes you may feel powerless, small, weak, or easily dominated. At other times, you may feel strong, overly responsible, guilty, or exasperated. When one member of a relationship is splitting, it often causes a complementary split in the other person. For instance, if a narcissist feels perfect, it can cause her partner to feel worthless and weak. It is a common experience among therapists who treat narcissism to feel ineffective, useless, or even incompetent when working with grandiose narcissists. Conversely, when working with vulnerable narcissists, it is common to feel superior, powerful, and clever.

The key to dealing with splitting is not allowing yourself to be swept up in the either/or mentality. Staying aware of how you are feeling in response to the narcissist is a useful strategy. Ask yourself, "How am I feeling right now? Do I feel big, powerful, annoyed, or guilty? Or, do I feel small, weak, wrong, or ashamed?" Noticing whether you are feeling idealized or devalued can help you understand how the narcissist is operating. It can also help you avoid losing a whole picture of yourself and the other person.

Partner or Ex-Partner

To a certain extent, many of the behaviors discussed in this chapter are normal in romantic relationships. People tend to idealize things when a relationship first begins. The "honeymoon period" can last anywhere from a few weeks to a few years. During this time, people tend to see the relationship as perfect. This fantasy of ideal love from an ideal partner is almost indistinguishable from the ways that narcissists fantasize about perfection. Many look to a new partner for narcissistic supply, seeking admiration, compliments, and reassurance that they are attractive and desired. Many people also experience strong feelings of jealousy during this period, imagining that others want to steal their newfound happiness.

When it comes to unhealthy narcissism, there are many ways that vanity can show up in romantic or ex-romantic relationships. Some narcissists pressure their partners to provide constant validation. Others use their partners as trophies or status symbols. In some relationships, sex and intimacy become problematic if the narcissistic partner doesn't feel admired and appreciated enough. In addition, jealousy can become a very toxic factor.

If you feel that idealization and devaluation are playing a problematic role in your relationship, you may need to confront the behaviors and challenge the perceptions of your partner. Again, the best way to do this is to wait for a neutral time when things are calm. Be sure to take responsibility for your feelings by phrasing things in terms of how you feel.

Perhaps most importantly, try to avoid dividing anyone up into good and bad parts (including yourself). Check in with yourself frequently to see how you are feeling. If things seem polarized, try to move back into the middle. For instance, if you realize that you are seeing your partner as a bully, try to remind yourself of the qualities you fell in love with. If you realize that you're feeling small and vulnerable, try to remember that you are a whole person who can also be strong.

Parent

People want their parents to admire and idealize them, which is why it can be especially difficult when parents are the ones seeking admiration. Parents who use their children to fulfill their own narcissistic needs represent a common theme in theories about narcissism. Whether or not it is intentional, inverting the natural parent-child relationship has devastating and long-lasting effects. If you're reading this book with a parent in mind, things have probably been this way for a long time. It's hard to confront the status quo, especially when you are trying to change relationship patterns that have been in place for years.

When it comes to making changes in a relationship, sometimes the bulk of the work needs to happen inside of you. Think about the ways that you participate in your parent's search for narcissistic supply. Do you respond to pressure by giving compliments that aren't genuine? Do you often feel obligated to let your parent have the spotlight? Do you sit uncomfortably through self-congratulatory monologues that remind you of feeling overlooked, marginalized,

Discussing Feelings

Feelings and thoughts are different. Feelings involve words like *sad, angry, happy,* and *disappointed*. Many people think they are talking about feelings when they are actually talking about thoughts and opinions. Saying something like "I feel like you're insensitive and rude" is actually a criticism. It is *not* discussing your feelings. One way to discuss feelings is to phrase comments using statements that follow this format: "When _____ happens, I feel _____." For example, you might say something like, "When you don't allow me to finish my thought, I feel frustrated and unimportant."

and ignored as a child? If so, you are actually participating in continuing a relationship pattern that is hurtful to you.

A theme throughout this book has been to confront problematic behavior without losing sight of yourself or the other person. Narcissists continually tear down boundaries between themselves and others. They seek to merge with the people they idealize, and try to throw away the people onto whom they project their own unwanted qualities. Narcissists are stymied by people who can remain grounded in their own self-worth. Remaining connected to your worth prevents splitting. This is the space you need to occupy to begin to make changes in any relationship with a narcissist, whether it is a lover, a friend, or even a parent. When you can find this middle ground, you will naturally resist the pulls to engage in hurtful relationship patterns.

Boss or Coworker

A certain amount of vanity is normal in a work environment, especially if it is a competitive atmosphere. Supervisors and managers want their employees to admire and respect them. People are often striving to do their best work, and sometimes coworkers can become envious of one another. Vanity becomes an issue when it is causing significant distress in your working relationship.

Although they may not like it, people often respect those who don't give in to pressure to behave in ways that aren't genuine. There is considerable pressure to conform to expectations at work. However, when you feel pressured to gratify the narcissistic needs of someone—whether it's a coworker, boss, or employee—it may be time to think about setting a boundary. Setting a boundary may mean having a private discussion with the problematic person or, in more extreme cases, discussing things with management or the human resources department. Whatever your specific situation, the most important piece involves learning to remain grounded in the face of your own internal reactions to the narcissistic behavior. The following section on healing activities may help.

Healing Techniques

The techniques in this chapter will focus on helping you remain grounded when dealing with projections, splitting, and other forms of emotional coercion.

Seeing Both Sides

Narcissists spend a lot of time fluctuating between extreme points of view. They see themselves and others as all good or all bad, idealized or devalued, perfect or worthless. When someone adopts an extreme position, he often pressures others into taking the opposite position. This exercise will help you see both sides of the equation when feelings run high and you begin to veer into black-and-white thinking.

With a pen and paper, spend some time thinking about yourself. Make three columns. Label the first column "Best." Label the second column "Worst." Label the third column "Most Likely." Take a look at yourself from a third-person perspective (i.e., from someone else's point of view). In the first column, list the ways that people might idealize you. Perhaps they think you are beautiful, smart, or privileged. Don't worry too much about being accurate. Just let your mind run wild. In the second column, list the things that others might despise about you. Perhaps they see you as selfish, inept, or ugly. Again, accuracy isn't the goal. In the third column, list the ways that people most likely see you. Perhaps they might see you as nice, generous, shy, or creative.

Now look back over your lists. Pay attention to the feelings that come up when you read the Best column. What are those feelings like? Where have you felt them before? Where in your body do you feel them? Do the same for the Worst column. Notice those feelings. Do they remind you of anything? Where in your body are they located?

These are the sorts of feelings to watch for when dealing with narcissistic behavior. When you feel the feelings associated with the Best column, you are being idealized. When you feel the feelings from the Bad column, you are being devalued. As you become more aware of your own internal reactions to narcissistic idealizations and devaluations, it gets easier to find your way back to the middle ground.

Noticing the Conceptualized Self, the Observing Self, and Self-as-Context

This can be a difficult concept to grasp, but it can be life-changing once you understand it. To put it simply, *you are not your thoughts.* The mind is a constant swirl of thoughts—many of which happen so quickly that you never even notice them. They can be extreme, upsetting, pleasurable, gentle, offensive, violent, or kind. Some happen frequently, while others may have only happened once or twice in your entire life. Many have yet to be thought. Some thoughts are about things in the world, and some are about other thoughts. Some thoughts are closely tied to specific people and situations in your life, while others are more broad and general.

Despite your ever-changing thoughts, there is a part of you that has always been the same. Close your eyes. Allow yourself to connect with your breath, settling into your body and the present moment. When you feel calm and centered, think back to your six-year-old self. Try to step into that little child and see the world through his or her eyes. Notice how it feels to be that version of yourself. Some things are dramatically different. However, some things are the same. There is a part of you that was present then, and is present now. This is what gives you a sense of unbroken continuity between the different stages of your life. This part of you is constant. It is unaffected by your thoughts.

Primarily, thoughts assign labels and solve problems. This ability works well when it's applied to problems in the outside world. It lets people figure out how to build houses, drive cars, and balance a checkbook. But that same label-making ability doesn't always help when applied to the self. When people label themselves, they create problems for their minds to solve. For example, your mind may label you as weak or stupid in response to a situation. This creates the problem of how to *not* be weak or stupid. Things can quickly get out of hand when a person identifies with her own self-labels.

This is what is meant by the term *conceptualized self*. There are an infinite number of possible conceptualized selves. Each person has hundreds, thousands, or even millions of them. For example, you might have a conceptualized self that is about having been bullied in fifth grade, one about the success of graduating from college, and one about having a successful career. Much of a person's psychological distress actually comes from identifying with his own self-directed thoughts. Suddenly, you are stupid, worthless, weak, or ugly. Rather than recognize these as labeled parts of yourself, you mistake them for your *actual* self.

In contrast, the part of you that has always been there, regardless of what was happening and how you felt, is the observing self. It is the part that watches your own experience. It defies labels because it simply watches your mind's attempts to label it. When people meditate, they are connecting with this larger self, watching their internal processes of labeling and problem solving while identifying with none of them.

Both of these parts exist in a context. They are both "you." One changes constantly with thoughts and feelings, the other is unchanging. If you pull back for an even broader perspective, you include the context in which both these parts exist as yet another aspect of self. This is called the self-as-context.

One way of thinking about these different parts of yourself is to imagine the sky. The sky is home to all sorts of activity: weather systems, clouds, birds, wind, rain, hurricanes. None of these things, on its own, *is* the sky. They are all parts of the sky. Even if you take them all together, they still don't add up to "the sky." The sky is the place where these things happen. It is the context in which weather occurs, in which birds fly, and in which the sun shines. In this example, the clouds and birds are thoughts and feelings while the sky itself is the self-as-context.

As another example, imagine a forest. Forests are teeming with life. Some of that life is pleasant to us, like flowers, deer, or babbling brooks. Other life in the forest is unpleasant to us, like mosquitoes, spiders, poison ivy, or snakes. People are like the forest. Everyone has parts to which they assign positive and negative labels, but those parts are balanced by the other objects in the forest. Everyone is home to many different selves. There are happy selves, angry selves, ambitious selves, and frightened selves. If you make the mistake of thinking that a single conceptualized self is the whole picture, then you mistake the forest for the trees.

How does all of this help you deal with narcissism? Narcissists have difficulty connecting with their observing self and their self-as-context. They are continually running from "bad" conceptualized selves and continually chasing "good" ones. They try to get rid of the bad ones by projecting them onto others. When you find yourself being pulled in one direction or another, try to remember that you transcend any particular label that your mind might assign. You are not good or bad. You are the place where thoughts like *good* and *bad* happen. You are the being that gives meaning to ideas like goodness and badness. You are also the being that watches your experiences. You've always been there, since the moment that you were born.

Conclusion

Narcissists are difficult to get along with. You're probably already familiar with the self-centeredness, grandiosity, vanity, and vulnerability that characterize this problematic personality style. You've been idealized, devalued, taken for granted, and taken advantage of. Where do you go from here?

Narcissism is a condition that robs people of their personhood. It reduces everyone (both the narcissist and the people they care about) to objects that are defined by superficial qualities. The only antidote is to do the hard work of finding the real people behind the projections. This book shared some insights into better understanding yourself and the narcissist in your life, and provided the information you need to make an informed choice about what to do with that relationship.

This book attempted to give you the tools to decode and unmask narcissistic behaviors. It discussed stories that illustrate how narcissistic traits can look in real-life scenarios, and reviewed exercises to help you clarify your thoughts, feelings, and values. It also covered setting boundaries, confronting and accepting vulnerability, and finding balance within yourself.

Narcissists use grandiosity as a defense against insecurity, shame, and vulnerability, attempting to offload
negative feelings onto others through denial and projection. Although the temptation is to throw those negative
feelings back at the narcissist, doing so only exacerbates
anger and tension. Instead of going to war with the narcissist's projections, being able to acknowledge and accept
your own vulnerabilities will allow you to remain centered
in response to narcissistic devaluation.

Self-centered behaviors like entitlement, low empathy,
and exploitation are traits narcissists use to make up for
deep feelings of impoverishment. On an emotional level,
narcissists are starving and desperate for your help. If you
let them, they will gobble up all of your resources, leaving
you to starve as well. Set boundaries to protect your emotional and psychological space. Be assertive, keeping in
mind the differences between aggressive, passive, and
assertive behavior. Perhaps most importantly, don't get too
attached to outcomes. All you can do is speak your truth.
If someone doesn't respect your boundaries, you always
have the choice to walk away.

Finally, with vanity, narcissists try to create a perfect outside to compensate for an emotionally chaotic inside. Using
the concept of splitting, narcissists tend to unconsciously
separate themselves and the world into categories of perfect and worthless, good and bad, idealized and devalued.
Since narcissists' extreme thoughts and feelings often
create complimentary extreme thoughts and feelings in

How Is Narcissism Treated?

Like any personality issue, it takes time to treat narcissism effectively. Treatment can last anywhere from six months to six years or longer, depending on the individual. This is because personality issues have deep roots that take time to uncover and work through. It's not just a simple matter of giving someone some new coping skills (although that is often a first step in the process). Patients need to be helped to see themselves and the world differently.

Treatment for narcissism involves identifying, interpreting, and confronting the patient's use of problematic defenses like grandiosity, self-centeredness, and vanity. The patient must be helped to recognize his use of these defenses and to see how they actually prevent intimacy and fulfillment. This aspect of treatment can be the work of several years.

As the defenses are gradually challenged and relinquished, the underlying vulnerabilities may begin to surface. This often feels like a crisis to the patient because it seems like things are actually getting worse. The patient must be helped to understand where the feelings of pain, isolation, dependency, and anxiety come from. The therapist helps the patient experience these feelings, providing mirroring and empathy to aid the patient in creating a new sense of self that is not based on splitting. Much like children use their parents, the patient uses the therapist's whole self to create his own whole self.

Throughout treatment, the patient must grieve. The tragedy of narcissism is that beneath the false self, there is a person who never lived. The narcissist's real self never came into being. Looking into the pain and grief that surrounds this issue is excruciating.

If treatment goes well, the patient will gradually develop a stable sense of self—one based on lived experience rather than positive or negative feedback from others. As this new self grows, the patient will rely on others less for narcissistic supply. At the same time, having a self allows the patient to see others as whole people, paving the way for empathy to develop. Narcissists are never fully "cured." They will always have a narcissistic personality style—meaning that, to some extent, their psychologies will always be organized around issues of self-esteem. However, this isn't necessarily a bad thing. Everyone has a personality style. People with narcissistic personality styles are often gifted performers, charismatic leaders, and even compassionate therapists.

others, it can help to monitor your own inner experience to avoid being pulled into splitting. Narcissism cuts people up into good and bad pieces. The best way to confront this is to approach things as a whole, complex person.

If you decide to continue working on your relationship with the narcissist in your life, consider enlisting support. Family and friends can be great resources when you need a reminder that you aren't alone. You might also consider talking to a therapist. Therapy isn't just for people with severe mental health issues. It can be a tremendous source of support when dealing with stressful situations. Therapists are trained to meet you where you are, offering appropriate and individually tailored feedback to help you better understand yourself and your situation. A good therapist will listen in an attentive and nonreactive way, providing feedback that gives you a feeling of being seen and understood. Sometimes, it takes a few tries before finding a good match.

If the narcissist in your life is open to the idea, she might also benefit from therapy. Just be careful not to use the idea of therapy as a weapon. It's easy to say things like, "You *really* need therapy!" or "You have *issues*. Why don't you go see a shrink?" These sorts of comments are really just ways of throwing negative projections back at the narcissist. It is counterproductive because it reinforces the stereotype that therapy is only for "crazy" people. It also stigmatizes seeking help as something shameful (and narcissists are not huge fans of feeling shame). Instead, wait for a calm moment and express your encouragement in an open and caring way. You might say, "You know, I hear you talking about how stressed you've been feeling lately. Have you considered getting some support from a therapist? I think talking to an expert might really help you feel better about things."

This journey began with the myth of Narcissus, who tragically fell in love with an ideal image of himself too perfect to ever exist in the real world. Equally tragic is the story of Echo, whose voice was never heard by the preoccupied Narcissus. While you may be playing the part of Echo at this moment, you don't have to allow yourself to be eclipsed by the Narcissus in your life. Although difficult, it is possible to work toward making enough space for both you and the other person to "show up" to each other. Even if the narcissist in your life isn't willing to make changes, you have the ability to make yourself better, give yourself the space and consideration that you deserve, and make sure that your voice is heard. Sometimes this is a journey that you can take *with* the narcissist in your life. Sometimes it isn't. Either way, don't lose sight of your right to be heard, respected, and seen.

References

American Psychiatric Association. *Diagnostic and Statistical Manual of Mental Disorders.* 5th ed. Arlington, VA: American Psychiatric Publishing, 2013.

Arble, E. P. "Evaluating the Psychometric Properties of the Hypersensitive Narcissism Scale: Implications for the Distinction of Covert and Overt Narcissism." Master's Thesis, Eastern Michigan University. 2008. Accessed October 12, 2015. commons.emich.edu /theses/236.

Ben-Porath, Y. *Interpreting the MMPI-2-RF.* Minneapolis: University of Minnesota Press, 2012.

Bennett, C. S. "Attachment Theory and Research Applied to the Conceptualization and Treatment of Pathological Narcissism." *Clinical Social Work Journal* 34, no. 1 (2006): 45–60.

Blatt, S. J., and K. N. Levy. "Attachment Theory, Psychoanalysis, Personality Development, and Psychopathology." *Psychoanalytic Inquiry* 23, no. 1 (2003): 104–152.

Britton, R. "Narcissistic Disorders in Clinical Practice." *Journal of Analytical Psychology* 49, no. 4 (2004): 477–490.

Bursten, B. "Some Narcissistic Personality Types." *International Journal of Psycho-analysis* 54 (1973): 287–300.

Chessick, R. *Psychology of the Self and the Treatment of Narcissism.* Northvale, NJ: Jason Aronson, 1985.

Cooper, A. M., and R. Michels. "Diagnostic and Statistical Manual of Mental Disorders, revised (DSM-III-R)." *American Journal of Psychiatry* 145, no. 10 (1988): 1300–1301.

Dickinson, K. A., and A. L. Pincus. "Interpersonal Analysis of Grandiose and Vulnerable Narcissism." *Journal of Personality Disorders* 17, no. 3 (2003): 188–207.

Emmons, R. A. "Factor Analysis and Construct Validity of the Narcissistic Personality Inventory." *Journal of Personality Assessment* 48, no. 3 (1984): 291–300.

Emmons, R. A. "Narcissism Theory and Measurement." *Journal of Personality and Social Psychology* 52, no. 1 (1987): 11–17.

Ettensohn, M. D. "The Relational Roots of Narcissism: Exploring Relationships between Attachment Style, Acceptance by Parents and Peers, and Measures of Grandiose and Vulnerable Narcissism." Doctoral dissertation, 2011. ProQuest (AAT 3515488).

Feintuch, B. "Adult Attachment, Narcissism, Shame, and Defensiveness." Dissertation, Michigan State University Department of Psychology, 1988.

Freud, S. *On Narcissism.* London: The Hogarth Press, 1914.

Gabbard, G. O. "Two Subtypes of Narcissistic Personality Disorder." *Bulletin of the Menninger Clinic* 53 (1989): 527–532.

Goldner-Vukov, M., and L. J. Moore. "Malignant Narcissism: From Fairy Tales to Harsh Reality." *Psychiatria Danubina* 22, no. 3 (2010), 392–405.

Harder, D. W., and S. J. Lewis. "The Assessment of Shame and Guilt." In *Advances in Personality Assessment*, edited by J. N. Butcher and C. D. Spielberger, 89–114. Hillsdale, NJ: Erlbaum, 1987.

"Haughty." Merriam-Webster Online. Accessed September 26, 2015. www.merriam-webster.com/dictionary/haughty.

Heiserman, A., and H. Cook. "Narcissism, Affect, and Gender: An Empirical Examination of Kernberg's and Kohut's Theories of Narcissism." *Psychoanalytic Psychology* 15, no. 1 (1998): 74–92.

Hendin, H. M., and J. M. Cheek. "Assessing Hypersensitive Narcissism: A Reexamination of Murray's Narcissism Scale." *Journal of Research in Personality* 31, no. 4 (1997): 588–599.

Hibbard, S. "Narcissism, Shame, Masochism, and Object Relations: An Exploratory Correlational Study." *Psychoanalytic Psychology* 9, no. 4 (1992): 489–508.

Holdren, M. "Causal Attributions among Overt and Covert Narcissism Subtypes for Hypothetical, Retrospective, and Prospective Events." Doctoral dissertation, 2004. ProQuest (AAT 3146467).

Horowitz, L. M., R. de Sales French, K. D. Wallis, D. L. Post, and E. Y. Siegelman. "The Prototype as a Construct in Abnormal Psychology." *Journal of Abnormal Psychology* 90, no. 6 (1981): 575–585.

Johnson, S. M. *Character Styles.* New York: W. W. Norton & Co., 1994.

Johnson, S. M. *Humanizing the Narcissistic Style.* New York: W. W. Norton & Co., 1987.

Kernberg, O. F. "Factors in the Psychoanalytic Treatment of Narcissistic Personalities." *Journal of the American Psychoanalytic Association* 18 (1970): 51–85.

Kernberg, O. F. "Further Contributions to the Treatment of Narcissistic Personalities." *International Journal of Psychoanalysis* 55 (1974): 215–240.

Kernberg, O. F. *Severe Personality Disorders.* New Haven, CT: Yale University Press, 1984.

Kohut, H. *The Analysis of the Self.* New York: International Universities Press, 1971.

Kohut, H. "Forms and Transformations of Narcissism." *Journal of the American Psychoanalytic Association* 14 (1966): 243–272.

Kohut, H. *The Restoration of the Self.* New York: International Universities Press, 1977.

Kohut, H., and E. S. Wolf. "The Disorders of the Self and Their Treatment: An Outline." *International Journal of Psychoanalysis* 59 (1978): 413–425.

Lewis, H. B. "Shame and Guilt in Neurosis." *Psychoanalytic Review* 58 (1971): 419–438.

Mahler, M. S. *On Human Symbiosis and the Vicissitudes of Individuation.* New York: International Universities Press, 1968.

Mahler, M. S. "Rapprochement Subphase of the Separation-Individuation Process." *Psychoanalytic Quarterly* 4 (1972): 487–506.

Masterson, J. F. *The Emerging Self: A Developmental, Self, and Object Relations Approach to the Treatment of the Closet Narcissistic Disorders of the Self.* New York: Bruner/Mazel, 1993.

Meyer, G. J., D. J. Viglione, J. L. Mihura, R. E. Erard, and P. Erdberg. *Rorschach Performance Assessment System: Administration, Coding, Interpretation, and Technical Manual.* Toledo, OH: Rorschach Performance Assessment System, LLC, 2011.

Miller, A. "Depression and Grandiosity as Related Forms of Narcissistic Disturbances." *International Review of Psycho-Analysis* 6 (1979): 62–76.

Miller, A. *The Drama of the Gifted Child.* New York: Basic Books, 1981.

Mollon, P. *The Fragile Self: The Structure of Narcissistic Disturbance and Its Therapy.* Northvale: Jason Aronson, 1993.

Montebarocci, O., P. Surcinelli, B. Baldaro, E. Trombini, and N. Rossi. "Narcissism Versus Proneness to Shame and Guilt." *Psychological Reports* 94, no. 3 (2004): 883–887.

Morrison, A. "The Eye Turned Inward: Shame and the Self." In *The Many Faces of Shame*, edited by D. Nathanson, 271–291. New York: Guilford Press, 1987.

Morrison, A. "Introduction." In *Essential Papers on Narcissism*, edited by A. Morrison, 1–11. New York: New York University, 1986.

Morrison, A. "Shame, Ideal Self, and Narcissism." *Contemporary Psychoanalysis* 19 (1983): 295–318.

Morrison, A. *Shame: The Underside of Narcissism.* New Jersey: The Analytic Press, 1989.

Morrison, A., and R. Stolorow. "Shame, Narcissism, and Intersubjectivity." In *The Widening Scope of Shame,* edited by M. Lansky and A. Morrison, 63–87. New Jersey: The Analytic Press, 1997.

Otway, L. J., and V. L. Vignoles. "Narcissism and Childhood Recollections: A Quantitative Test of Psychoanalytic Predictions." *Personality and Social Psychology Bulletin* 32, no. 1 (2006): 104–116.

PDM Task Force. *Psychodynamic Diagnostic Manual.* Silver Spring, MD: Alliance of Psychoanalytic Organizations, 2006.

Piers, G., and M. B. Singer. *Shame and Guilt: A Psychoanalytic and a Cultural Study.* New York: W. W. Norton & Co, 1971.

Pulver, S. "Narcissism: The Term and the Concept." *Journal of the American Psychoanalytic Association* 18 (1970): 319–341.

Raskin, R., and C. Hall. "A Narcissistic Personality Inventory." *Psychological Reports* 45, no. 2 (1979): 590.

Raskin, R., and C. Hall. "The Narcissistic Personality Inventory: Alternate Form Reliability and Further Evidence of Construct Validity." *Journal of Personality Assessment* 45 (1981): 159–162.

Raskin, R., and J. Novacek. "An MMPI Description of the Narcissistic Personality." *Journal of Personality Assessment* 53, no. 1 (1989): 66–80.

Raskin, R. and H. Terry. "A Principal-Components Analysis of the Narcissistic Personality Inventory and Further Evidence of Its Construct Validity." *Journal of Personality and Social Psychology* 54 (1988): 890–902.

Reich, A. "Pathologic Forms of Self-Esteem Regulation. *Psychoanalytic Study of the Child* 15 (1960): 215–232.

Robins, R. W., J. L. Tracy, and P. R. Shaver. "Shamed into Self-Love: Dynamics, Roots, and Functions of Narcissism." *Psychological Inquiry* 12, no. 4 (2001): 230–236.

Schurman, C. L. "Social Phobia, Shame and Hypersensitive Narcissism." Doctoral dissertation, 2000. ProQuest (AAT 9986811).

Smolewska, K., and K. L. Dion. "Narcissism and Adult Attachment: A Multivariate Approach." *Self and Identity* 4 (2005): 59–68.

Strack, S. *Essentials of Millon Inventories Assessment, Third Edition*. Hoboken, NJ: John Wiley & Sons, 2008.

Teicholz, J. G. "A Selective Review of the Psychoanalytic Literature on Theoretical Conceptualizations of Narcissism." *Journal of the American Psychoanalytic Association* 26 (1978): 831–861.

Vitek, J. A. "Aggression and Differentiation of Self in Narcissistic Subtypes." Doctoral dissertation, 2000. ProQuest (AAT 9970787).

Wink, P. "Two Faces of Narcissism." *Journal of Personality and Social Psychology* 61, no. 4 (1991): 590–597.

Winnicott, D. W. "Ego Distortion in Terms of the True and False Self." *The Maturational Process and the Facilitating Environment*. New York: International Universities Press, 1960.

Winnicott, D. W. *The Maturational Processes and the Facilitating Environment*. New York: International Universities Press, 1965.

Winnicott, D. W. *Playing and Reality*. London: Tavistock Publications, 1971.

Resources

PSYCHCENTRAL.COM/QUIZZES/NARCISSISTIC.HTM An online test for measuring traits of grandiose narcissism, adapted from the Narcissistic Personality Inventory (NPI).

BLOGS.SCIENTIFICAMERICAN.COM/BEAUTIFUL-MINDS/23-SIGNS-YOUE28099RE-SECRETLY-A-NARCISSIST-MASQUERADING-AS-A-SENSITIVE-INTROVERT/ An online test for measuring traits of vulnerable narcissism.

WWW.NMHA.ORG Mental Health America's website, containing numerous articles and resources.

THERAPISTS.PSYCHOLOGYTODAY.COM/RMS/ *Psychology Today*'s online therapist finder. Use this tool to locate a therapist near you.

WWW.PSYCHOLOGYTODAY.COM/BLOG/FULFILLMENT-ANY-AGE/201408/8-WAYS-HANDLE-NARCISSIST A *Psychology Today* article discussing strategies for coping with narcissistic individuals.

HUMANIZING THE NARCISSISTIC STYLE BY STEPHEN JOHNSON, PHD A book written for professionals, but accessible for anyone familiar with psychological concepts.

THE DRAMA OF THE GIFTED CHILD BY ALICE MILLER A poignant account of the origins of narcissistic disturbances in children.

WWW.DRETTENSOHN.COM/NARCISSISTIC-PERSONALITY-DISORDER/ An article by Mark Ettensohn, Psy.D., that explains narcissistic personality disorder (NPD) for laypersons.

WWW.DRETTENSOHN.COM/NARCISSISM-AND-THE-NEVER-ENDING-PURSUIT-OF-SELF-WORTH/ An article by Mark Ettensohn, Psy.D., that discusses narcissistic conflicts.

WWW.REDDIT.COM/R/RAISEDBYNARCISSISTS An online support forum for individuals raised by narcissistic parents.

About the Author

Mark Ettensohn is a clinical psychologist in Sacramento, California. He specializes in treating narcissism and providing psychotherapy for chronic emotional, psychological, and relational distress. He graduated with a doctorate in clinical psychology from the Wright Institute in Berkeley, California, where his dissertation research investigated developmental factors that cause grandiose and vulnerable narcissism. Dr. Ettensohn has also authored and contributed to several articles on the subject for both laypersons and professionals.

You can learn more about Dr. Ettensohn by visiting his website at www.DrEttensohn.com.

About the Foreword Author

Jane Simon, M.D., is a graduate of Barnard College and Temple Medical School. A psychiatrist in practice on the Upper West Side of Manhattan, she writes a biweekly blog, www.drsimonsays.blogspot .com, which has been syndicated by *The Huffington Post*. A book of poems, *Incisions*, describes her experience as a forensic pathologist that helped her transition to psychiatry. With the great cartoonist Jim Whiting, she penned *The Cabala of the Animals* and *A Toolbox of Paradoxes*, that include playful cartoons and epigrams. *A Toolbox of Blogs: Integrating Psyche and Society* is a print edition of online blogs from 2011 through 2014. She is working on a memoir tentatively titled *Red Diaper Daughter*.

Index

A

Abandonment
   anxiety over, 137
   in vulnerable narcissists, 75
Abusive behavior, 9, 102
Acting above the rules, 48
Admiration, need for, 127, 134, 135–144
   boasting or showing off in, 143
   as constant, 8
   excessiveness in, 17
   exhibitionistic behavior in, 142–143
   fishing for compliments in, 142
   fueling versus defusing in,
     140–141, 143–144
   real-life scenarios in, 135–137,
     140–141, 143–144
   reasons for, 137, 139–140
   unconsciousness and, 138–139
Advantage, pressing of, 101–102
Aggressive behavior, 107–108, 109, 112
Always being right, 49
Anger, 41
   grandiosity and, 74
   vulnerability and, 123
Antisocial personality disorder, 67
Antisocial traits, 30
Antoinette, Marie, 57–58
Anxiety, 13, 25, 50, 89
   abandonment and, 137
Arrogance, 11, 53–61
   examples of, 57–59
   fueling versus defusing, 56, 59–61
   real-life scenarios and, 53–55,
     56, 59–61
   reasons behind, 55–56
Assertiveness, 106–107, 112
Assurance, constant need for, 8

Attention, need for, 134
Authentic self, 28–29, 100
   lack of, 7

B

Batman, 24
Beauty, 17
   presenting image of, 8
Beauty and the Beast, 23–24, 82
   Gaston, 23–24, 82
Behavior
   abusive, 9, 102
   aggressive, 107–108, 109
   assertive, 107–108, 109, 112
   dismissive, 58
   exhibitionistic, 142–143
   exploitative, 9, 106
   high-handed, 57–58
   inconsiderate, 91
   judgmental, 58–59
   passive, 107
   self-centered, 165
   self-serving, 106–118
Bias, gender, 25
Bill of Rights, 78
Bitterness, feelings of, 150–151
Black-and-white thinking, 159–160
Blame, 74
   issuing, 9
Boasting, 39, 143
Borderline personality
   disorder, 25, 89
Boundaries, setting, 105, 106–109,
   113, 117, 158, 165
Bragging, 39
Brilliance, 17
Bullying, 44, 57, 108, 140

C

Cheating, 102
Children
    development of, 127–128
    parental exploitation of, 98
    used, 28, 98
Clarification of values, 113, 116
Clinical depression, 93
Comfort, difficulty providing, 90
Compliments, need for, 127, 142
Conceptualized self, 160–163
Condescension, 53
Conditional love, 79
Co-occurring symptoms, 14
Core values, 116
Cozy, getting, with
    discomfort, 116–118
Criticism, sensitivity to, 103

D

Deceptiveness, 30
Defensive self-sufficiency, 22
Defensive stonewalling, 103
Defiance, 60
Defusing, 41–43
    arrogance and, 56, 59–61
    empathy and, 92–94
    entitlement and, 82–83
    envy and, 149, 151–152
    exploitation and, 103–105
    haughtiness and, 56, 59–61
    personal exceptionalism
        and, 50–52
Denial, 34
Dependency
    entitlement and, 79
    vulnerability and, 75
Depression, 13, 25, 50, 89, 92
    clinical, 93
Destabilization, 153
Devaluation, fluctuation between

idealization and, 131–132
*Diagnostic and Statistical Manual
    of Mental Disorders* (DSM), 14
    fifth edition of, 14
Diagnostic interviews, 14
Difficulty providing comfort, 90
Discomfort, getting cozy
    with, 116–118
Disdain, treating narcissists with, 10
Dismissive behavior, 58
Disorientation, feelings of, 133
Downloading, illegal, 81
*The Drama of the Gifted
    Child* (Miller), 98

E

Echo, myth of, 12–13, 42–43, 169
Egocentrism, 38
Emotional coercion, 57
Emotional maturity, 38
Empathy, 8, 11, 14, 17, 30, 106
    attunement in, 7
    difficulties providing comfort, 90
    distinguishing between
        sympathy and, 85
    fueling versus defusing, 92–94
    inconsiderate behavior and, 91
    invisibility and, 91
    kicking others when down, 90
    mirroring and, 88–89,
        91, 92, 99, 100
    real-life scenarios in, 86–88, 92–94
    reasons behind, 88–89, 91–92
Entitlement, 11, 76–84, 106
    dependency and, 79
    feeling put upon in, 80
    forms of, 76
    freeloading and, 81
    fueling versus defusing
        and, 82–83
    making of personal

exceptions and, 81
real-life scenarios in, 77–78, 82–84
reasons for, 78–79, 82
self-absorption and, 80–81
sense of, 17
Envy, feelings of, 17, 145–152
bitterness and, 150–151
fueling versus defusing
in, 149, 151–152
life as unfair and, 150
obsession and preoccupation
and, 151
real-life scenarios
and, 145–147, 149, 151–152
reasons for, 147–149
Ettensohn, Mark, 177
Exhibitionism, 142–143
Exploitation, 9, 95–105, 106
abusing power differential in, 102
fueling versus defusing
in, 103–105
overt, 95
pressing advantage in, 101–102
real-life scenarios
and, 96–97, 103–105
reasons for, 98–100
setting boundaries in, 105
using others in, 101

F
Fairness, 101–102
False self, 27, 99, 123, 129, 130, 167
mask of, 8
Famous, fantasies of being, 131
Fantasies, preoccupation
with, 124–134
examples of, 131–132
real-life scenarios in, 125–127,
130, 132–134
reasons for, 127–130
Fear in grandiose narcissists, 73

Feedback, need for constant, 129
Feeling put upon, 80
Feelings
of bitterness, 150–151
discussing, 157
of disorientation, 133
of insecurity, 35
of obsession, 51
50–50 partnership, 64
Fishing for compliments, 142
Flattering, 84
Freeloading, 81
Freud, Sigmund, 18–19
Friends, pressuring of, 81
Front-loading, 109–110
Frustration, 22
Fueling, 41–43
arrogance and, 56, 59–61
empathy and, 92–94
entitlement and, 82–83
envy and, 149, 151–152
exploitation and, 103–105
haughtiness and, 56, 59–61
personal exceptionism
and, 50–52

G
Games, cheating in, 102
Gender biases, 25
Grandiosity, 14, 16, 23–24, 29,
33–71, 34
anger in, 74
arrogant, haughty behavior
and attitudes in, 53–61
blame in, 74
crisis in, 74
dealing with, 62–71
as defense, 165
denial and, 34
dismissive behavior in, 41
façade of perfection in, 73,

121–122
    fear, shame, and self-
      loathing in, 73
    healing techniques in, 68–71
    parenting in, 65–66
    personal exceptionalism in, 44–52
    polarized thinking in, 154
    projection and, 34
    protection of narcissist and, 73
    rage in, 41
    real-life scenarios in, 36–37,
      41–43, 44–46, 50–52,
      53–55, 56, 59–61
    responding instead of
      reacting, 63–64
    romantic relationships
      in, 64–65
    self-importance in, 36–43
    traits in, 16
    unrealistic ideas in, 124
    vanity in, 121–122
    work relationships in, 66–68
Grandstanding, 39
Guilt, 92
Guilt-tripping, 84

H

Haughtiness, 53–61
    examples of, 57–59
    fueling versus defusing, 56,
      59–61
    real-life scenarios
      and, 53–55, 56, 59–61
    reasons behind, 55–56
Healing techniques
    in grandiosity, 68–71
    in self-serving behavior, 113–118
    in vanity, 159–163
Healthy narcissism, 20
High-handed behavior, 57–58

Histrionic personality disorder, 25
Hopelessness, 92
Houston, Whitney, 18
Humanizing the Narcissistic Style
    (Johnson), 98, 129
Human psychology, dimensions of, 20
Hyperfocus, 80
Hypersensitive Narcissism
    Scale (HDNS), 13, 15
Hypochondriasis, 139
Hysterical personality, 25

I

Idealization, fluctuation between
    devaluation and, 131–132
Ideal love, 17
Ideal self, 122
Impoverishment, 145
Inadequacy, protection from, 33
Inconsideration, 40, 91
Incuriousness, 40
Individuation, 129
Insecurity
    feelings of, 35
    protection from, 33
Intergenerational transmission, 50
Interpersonally exploitative, 17
Invisible, making others feel, 91

J

Johnson, Stephen, 33, 98, 129
Joker, 24
Judgmental behavior, 58–59

K

Kernberg, Otto, 22, 23
Kicking others when down, 90
Kohut, Heinz, 22, 23

L

Life, unfairness of, 150
Love
conditional, 79
parental, 79
of self, 18
Luthor, Lex, 26

M

Mahler, Margaret, 127
Malignant narcissist, 9
Manipulativeness, 30
Maslow, Abraham, 80–81
Meditation, mindfulness, 68–70
Men, narcissistic personality
disorder in, 25
Miller, Alice, 98
Millon Clinical Multiphasic Inventory,
3rd Edition (MCMI-III), 15
Mindfulness meditation, 68–70
Minnesota Multiplicand Personality
Inventory, 2nd Edition, Restructured
Form (MMPI-2-RF), 15
Mirroring, empathy
and, 88–89, 91, 92, 99, 100
Mocking, 57

N

Name-calling, 57
Name-dropping, 48
Narcissism
antisocial personality traits in, 67
core of, 26–27
defined, 12–13, 164
diagnosis of, 13, 14–18
empathizing with, 11
as gender neutral, 25
grandiose, 23–24, 29
healthy, 20
as high achieving, 7
leaving relationship, 21–22

malignant, 9
need to prove themselves, 7–8
origin of term, 7, 12
personality traits reflecting, 15–18
phallic, 25
primary, 20
reasons for attraction to, 30–31
secondary, 19
treating with disdain, 10
treatment for, 166–167
types of, 22–26
unhealthy, 155
vulnerable, 24, 29–30
Narcissistic personality
disorder (NPD), 7, 13
measuring symptoms of, 15
in men, 25
roots of, 8
Narcissistic Personality
Inventory (NPI), 13, 15
Narcissistic rage, 74
Narcissistic supply, 38, 40, 156
Narcissists
difficulty in getting along with, 164
as self-centered, 73
Narcissus, myth of, 7, 12–13,
28, 42–43
Negativity, meeting, with negativity, 8
No, saying, 9, 114–115

O

Observing self, 160–163
Obsession, feelings of, 151
On Narcissism (Freud), 19
Others
dependency on, 75
exploitation of, 101
invisibility in, 91
kicking, when down, 90
self-esteem and, 101, 127
Overt exploitation, 95

P

Panic attacks, 13
Parental exploitation of children, 98
Parental love, 79
Parenting, 20
    in grandiose behavior, 65–66
    in self-serving behavior, 111–112
    vanity and, 156–158
Passive aggression, 57
Passive behavior, 107
Perfection, 35, 124
    façade of, in grandiose
      narcissists, 73
    presenting image of, 8
Personal exceptionalism, 44–52, 81
    examples of, 48–49
    fueling versus defusing, 50–52
    real-life scenarios
      and, 44–46, 50–52
    reasons behind, 47
Personal hypocrisy, 48
Personality disorders, 21
    characteristics of, 13
    treatment of, 13
Personal space, 83
Phallic narcissism, 25
Phobias, 13
Pleading, 84
Polarized thinking, 9
    vanity and, 154
Potter, Harry, 26
Power, 17
Power differential, abusing a, 102
Praise, need for, 127, 134
Preoccupation
    with certain people, 151
    with fantasies, 124–134
Pressing advantage, 101–102
Prima donna, behaving like a, 39
Primary narcissism, 20
Problematic personality traits, 152

Process, 60
Projection, 34, 133
Pseudo-masculinity, 25
Psychodynamic Diagnostic Manual, 92

R

Rage, 41, 103
    narcissistic, 74
Rapprochement subphase of
    separation-individuation,
    128, 129–130, 137
Reacting, 63–64
Real-life scenarios
    arrogance and haughtiness
      and, 53–55, 56, 59–61
    empathy and, 86–88, 92–94
    entitlement and, 77–78, 82–84
    envy, feelings of
      and, 145–147, 149, 151–152
    exploitation and, 96–97, 103–105
    in grandiosity, 36–37, 41–43,
      44–46, 50–52, 53–55, 56,
      59–61
    in need for admiration,
      135–137, 140–141, 143–144
    personal exceptionalism
      and, 44–46, 50–52
    in preoccupation with fantasies,
      125–127, 130, 132–134
    self-importance and, 36–37, 41–43
    in self-serving behavior, 77–78,
      82–84, 86–88, 92–94, 96–97,
      103–105
    vanity and, 125–127, 130, 132–134,
      135–137, 140–141, 143–144,
      145–147, 149, 151–152
Reassurances, 137
    need for, 127
Reich, Wilhelm, 25
Rejection in vulnerable narcissists, 75

Resentment, 41
Responding, 63–64
Reverse psychology, 103–105
Ridicule, 41
Ridiculing appearance, 57
Right, always being, 49
Rolling with the resistance, 66
Romantic relationships
    grandiosity and, 64–65
    self-serving behavior and, 109–110
    vanity and, 154–166
Rorschach Personality Assessment
    System (R-PAS), 15
Rules, acting above the, 48

S

Scapegoating, 55–56
Secondary narcissism, 19
Seeing both sides, 159–160
Self
    conceptualized, 160–163
    observing, 160–163
Self-absorption in entitlement, 80–81
Self-actualization, 80
Self-aggrandizement, 25
Self-as-context, 160–163
Self-assurance, 45
Self-care, 116
Self-centered behaviors, 165
Self-doubt, 60
Self-esteem, 13, 80
    dependency on others for, 127
    developing healthy sense of, 7
    fluctuations between high
        and low, 131
    needs in, 22–23
    using others as sources of, 101
    in vulnerable narcissists, 75
Self-importance
    real-life scenarios
        and, 36–37, 41–43

Self-importance, grandiose
    sense of, 16
Selfishness, 11
Self-loathing, 73
Self-serving behavior, 16–17, 73–75, 84
    clarification of values in, 113, 116
    core values in, 116
    dealing with, 106–118
    entitlement in, 76–84
    exploitation in, 95–105
    getting cozy with discomfort
        in, 116–115
    healing techniques in, 113–118
    lack of empathy in, 85–94
    parent-child relationships
        in, 111–112
    real-life scenarios in, 77–78,
        82–84, 86–88, 92–94,
        96–97, 103–105
    romantic relationships
        and, 109–110
    saying no, 114–115
    setting boundaries in, 106–109,
        113, 117
    traits in, 16–17
    work relationships in, 112
Self-sufficiency, 127
Self-worth, 157
Sensitivity to criticism, 103
Separation-individuation,
    rapprochement subphase
    of, 128, 129–130, 137
Shame, 49
    feelings of, 35
    grandiosity and, 73
    protection from, 33
    vulnerability and, 123
Showing off, 143
Sides, seeing both, 159–160
Simon, Jane, 9, 177
Splitting, 130, 132–134

need for admiration and, 141
vanity and, 125, 153, 154, 158, 165
Standards, having
unreasonably high, 40
Stonewalling, defensive, 103
Substance abuse, 13, 50
Success, 17
presenting image of, 8
unrealistic ideas about, 124–125
Superman, 26
Sympathy, distinguishing
between empathy and, 85

T

Talking down, 107
Tantrum, throwing of, 84, 133–134
Thinking
black-and-white, 159–160
polarized, 9, 154
Trauma, 50

U

Ultimatums, issuing, 9
Unconsciousness, 138–139
in partner choice, 59–61
Unfairness of life, 150
Unhealthy narcissism, 155
Used children, 28, 98

V

Values
clarification of, 113, 116
core, 116
Vanity, 17–18, 121–163
admiration in, 135–144
conceptualized self,
observing self, and self-
as-context in, 160–163

dealing with, 153–163
feelings of envy in, 145–152
healing techniques in, 159–163
parent-child relationships
and, 156–158
polarized thinking and, 154
preoccupation with
fantasies in, 124–134
real-life scenarios and, 125–127,
130, 132–134, 135–137, 140–141,
143–144, 145–147, 149, 151–152
romantic relationships
and, 154–166
seeing both sides in, 159–160
splitting in, 125, 153, 154, 158, 165
traits in, 17–18
work relationships and, 158
Voldemort, 26
Vulnerability, 24, 29–30, 33–34, 35
abandonment in, 75
dependency on others and, 75
exploring, 70–71
false self in, 123
focus on imperfections in, 124
polarized thinking in, 154
rage in, 41
rejection in, 75
self-esteem and, 75
shame and anger in, 123

W

Winnicott, Donald, 89
Work relationships
grandiosity and, 66–68
self-serving behavior and, 112
vanity and, 158
Worthlessness, 92, 124

CPSIA information can be obtained
at www.ICGtesting.com
Printed in the USA
BVOW07s1500051116

466434BV00003B/3/P